Redeeming ATTACHMENT

A Counselor's Guide to
Facilitating Attachment to
God and Earned Security

Kendall Hunt
publishing company

Anita M. Knight, Ph.D.
Gary A. Sibcy II, Ph.D.
Liberty University

MW01129837

Cover image © Shutterstock.com

Kendall Hunt
publishing company

www.kendallhunt.com
Send all inquiries to:
4050 Westmark Drive
Dubuque, IA 52004-1840

Published in the United States of America

Contents

Acknowledgments

We would like to thank our clients and our students who have been an inspiration to us throughout the years with their resilience and willingness to seek growth. We would also like to thank Curtis Ross and Kendall Hunt Publishing for their efforts to make this book possible during this time and season.

Special thanks to Edwin Parker for transcribing many pages of this manuscript from its previous handwritten format and for helping compile the chapter summaries in order to provide concise summaries of content for our readers.

Heartfelt thanks to Kendyl DeCourcy, our editor, who has worked hard to review the text and ensure that it adheres to Grice's Maxims of collaborative communication.

We would also like to thank Dr. Tim Clinton for his belief in and support of this book, and for his inspiration and support.

In addition, we would like to thank CBSP researchers that have inspired our work, specifically Dr. Jennifer Kim Penberthy and Dr. James McCullough. Pioneers in attachment theory such as John Bowlby, the Father of Attachment, and his subsequent proponents of the work and theory Mary Ainsworth, Mary Main and Bob Marvin as well as many other colleagues writing and researching on the topic, have provided many of the sources used in this text and we thank them for carrying the torch forward and continuing the research. We would also like to give special thanks for Mary Main, Erik Hesse, and Naomi Gribneau for their work to keep the AAI certification training available and the countless hours they spend managing the reliability testing process. We have learned much about what to look for in the attachment dynamics we see with our clients.

We remain eternally thankful for our Redeeming Attachment Figure, God, and our Heavenly Father. We appreciate the opportunity He has afforded us to share what He has put on our hearts and minds. We are also thankful for our families for their support and encouragement as well, and for all that they have taught us about attachment on a personal level.

We would like to dedicate this writing to our Heavenly Father, and my (Anita's) beloved "Mims" (Grandmother) Ida Molina-Zinam, Ph.D. She is celebrating her 90th birthday September 19, 2017. She is an inspiration to all around her and seeks to always spread the love of Christ with all those that she encounters. Happy Birthday, Mims! Thank you for sharing the legacy of the Father's Heart.

About the Authors

ANITA M. KNIGHT, PH.D.

Anita M. Knight, Ph.D. is an Associate Professor of Counseling and a Licensed Professional Counselor (LPC) in the Department of Counselor Education and Family Studies at Liberty University. Dr. Knight teaches in the CACREP accredited clinical mental health counseling program and is the first place recipient of the Chancellor's Award for Teaching Excellence. Knight earned her doctorate in Counselor Education and Supervision and her MA in Community Counseling from Regent University. Knight is also certified as a highly reliable coder of the Adult Attachment Interview (AAI) through Mary Main and Eric Hesse's UC Berkeley AAI coder certification program.

GARY A. SIBCY II, PH.D.

Gary A. Sibcy II, Ph.D. is a Licensed Clinical Psychologist (LCP). He specializes in attachment based interventions and treatment for chronic depression. He is a Professor of Counseling in the doctoral program of Counselor Education and Supervision at Liberty University. He has authored the text "Attachments" together with Dr. Tim Clinton and has served as a pre-conference speaker for the American Association of Christian Counselors as well has specialized training in Cognitive Behavioral Analysis System of Psychotherapy (CBASP) and the Adult Attachment Interview (AAI).

Foreword

The special bond between a parent and child is undeniable, I remember when my daughter Megan was born . . . She had me wrapped around her finger from the day I first laid eyes on her. Truth is that she still does to this day! The love and trust that a child has for his or her mother or father is quite amazing. God wired us this way, but when that attachment bond is broken, or is never present in the first place, it can have devastating effects on the child that can last well into adulthood. Attachment/relationship wounds go deep in the soul and often affect and infect how we do or don't do relationships.

My colleagues and friends, Dr. Gary Sibcy and Dr. Anita Knight, have come together to write a powerful work to help us more effectively minister and offer wise counsel to those with attachment wounds. Using cutting-edge research on attachment, they have broken down a wealth of information into understandable language and ideas about the pathways to God and how we attach to Him in adaptive or maladaptive-broken ways.

When Dr. Sibcy, Dr. Knight, and I made the decision to invest years of our lives and countless hours of our professional careers in researching and teaching on attachment, we knew we were dedicating ourselves to a demanding task. We had no idea just how deep and wide our research would take us. The more we learned about attachment, the more we saw how it touched virtually every area of the lives of those around us.

I love the story of 'Grace' woven throughout this book. Like Grace, we all deeply need grace. Our brokenness doesn't have to define us. No matter what a person goes through in childhood, impacting their attachment style, the grace offered by our relational and loving Heavenly Father can redeem even the darkest past. Our dependence on God fuels true independence in life. When we get our eyes off of him, storm clouds gather.

In these pages, you will also learn how attachment relates to psychopathology, and how chronic depression and attachment injuries are linked. Gary and Anita also describe behavioral patterns that maintain chronic depression, how strategies used to treat depression will also move a person towards a secure autonomous attachment style.

Alternating between groundbreaking research and powerful stories, the narrative feel of the book makes it both a compelling and informative read. We all could benefit from learning more about attachment, both in understanding those we care for and interact with, but also in understanding a little more about ourselves. But in my opinion, the most important part of this book is the section on God Attachment. Nothing in life is more important than our relationship with God, but our attachment style can impact what we believe about God's love for us. Once we establish God as our secure base, the safety and security that result are unparalleled.

Life is so full of brokenness. Every day and in every way people are waiting for someone to hear them, to help them, and to be there for them. G.K. Chesterton once wrote, "There's a lot of difference between listening and hearing." Our job is not to just hear their stories but to listen. Listen and help. My prayer is that you will take some time to allow this work to sink in and I pray that God will use it in a powerful way.

—Tim Clinton, Ph.D.

Contributed by Tim Clinton. © Kendall Hunt Publishing Company

Part I

Introduction to Attachment Concepts

CHAPTER 1
The Case for Grace

"He has made everything appropriate in its time.
He has also set eternity in their heart, yet so that man
will not find out the work which God has done
from the beginning even to the end."

— *Ecclesiastes 3:11*

Grace was eight years old, she had long auburn hair, and brown eyes that had a special twinkle. Grace also had a smile that would warm your heart. She was very close with her grandmother and they used to snuggle up and read books together. Even though her grandmother was sick and not able to get around much, she loved to share books with Grace.

One day she told Grace that she was ready to go home to heaven. Grace protested, "No, Grandma, don't leave me! Please don't go!" Grandma went on to explain to Grace that eventually it would be her time and that she was looking forward to spending eternity with her Savior. Grace's eyes filled with tears, the thought of losing her beloved Grandma was too much to bear, so, she began using her creativity and began negotiating. She asked, "Grandma, will you wait for me so we can go together?"

Her Grandma replied, "No, honey, I will not be able to do that." Grace cried, and her Grandmother comforted her with the concept of heaven and the idea that Jesus is there. Grace had never heard much of this "Jesus."

Her Grandmother went on to share the story of the crucifixion explaining to Grace that Jesus died on the cross for her sins and took the punishment for her. Grace felt amazed and with awe and wonder asked more about this Jesus that was willing to take her punishment. She knew she wanted to know him more. Her grandmother was happy to tell her all about him! Her Grandma had a nail attached to the railing of her bed with a string, and Grace asked, "Grandma, what is this nail for? Aren't' you afraid it is going to poke you?!" Grace exclaimed.

"No, I am not afraid, Honey" Her grandmother answered gently. "The reason this nail is here is for the times when I'm asleep all night and I am dreaming about running or dancing, and then I wake up in the morning and realize that I have no legs" (you see Grandmother had no legs as both were amputated due to a chronic illness), "and when I think the pain is too much to bear, I look at this nail, and it reminds me that Jesus died on the cross, had these nails hammered through his hands for me and my sins! I think of Jesus' suffering, then all of a sudden, the pain is not too much to bear!" Grace was touched and amazed that anyone could love her so much as to take her punishment to the point of death and thus, that night, she began her relationship with Jesus through her Grandmother's introduction.

Eventually, Grace's grandmother's time came and she passed away, and Grace's heart was broken. Grace still reports missing her even more than a decade later, and still tears up when she shares how special their relationship was. However, she cherishes the memories that she has of their relationship and the lessons that she learned. Grace also reports that although she would do anything to have her grandmother back and misses her greatly, she believes that her grandmother is now in heaven, with legs, dancing!

Grace did not realize it until later, but when invited to reflect on this attachment relationship and how it impacted her adult personality, she realized her grandmother had given her a template for suffering and grief. Now, she recalls, teary eyed, the nail, and how keeping in mind Jesus' great sacrifice and love, nothing is too much to bear. As Grace reflects on what her Grandmother taught her, she realizes her Grandmother put suffering into perspective. Her Grandmother had given her a book for Christmas the year before she passed, that told the story of Jesus and she had signed the inside cover, "My Darling granddaughter, Grace. Learn well about Jesus. Love, Grandmother."

Due to her Grandmother's influence, Grace spent her life learning about and loving Jesus and was filled with gratitude for her Grandma and the time they had together. As a matter of fact, when Grace contemplates how she learned what love is, she believes her Grandmother was among the first to show her. If asked about her loss and how she makes sense of it, Grace's perspective is highly valuing (Tennyson, 1850), "It is better to have loved and lost, than never to have loved at all." *The warmth, support, and love of Christ is something that Grace will never lose, and these were enduring gifts that her grandmother gave to her that serve as a source of comfort to her even today.* You and I have access to this same enduring gift, (and we will discuss more on how to pursue this enduring love in Chapter 10: Seeking Proximity to the Divine Attachment Figure). Though Grace's Grandmother died years ago, Grace will still recall the love and tenderness they shared and the introduction to a lifelong love affair with her Savior who is eternal.

THE PURPOSE OF THIS BOOK

"Although the world is full of suffering, it is also full of the overcoming of it."

—Helen Keller

© anat chant/Shutterstock.com

This previous passage was part of Grace's story, part of her personal relationship history, which in this text we'll call her attachment history or her attachment story. Early relationships with caregivers such as parents and grandparents are referred to as "attachment" relationships. Many of our clients, students and supervisees, like Grace, have experienced tremendous love and pain throughout their attachment histories. Although we wish that we could have been the person they needed in the moment they needed us, and could have helped protect and buffer them from the pain of the attachment injury before it happened, sadly we could not. *However, we have entered their story for a time such as now. There is hope for redemption, and thus the Lord put it on our hearts to share the research based clinical tools and spiritual tools available to help people make sense of their attachment histories and go on to write an ending that is different than the beginning.* In the words of one of our favorite Christian apologists, C.S. Lewis, *"You can't go back and change the beginning, but you can start where you are and change the ending."* How our clients make sense of their stories is very important. I heard Dan Siegel speak at an Attachment conference at Harvard a few years ago, where he spoke about the neural integration that can take place when people recall these experiences and make sense of them with an empathic other, such as a counselor.

The purpose of this text is to reveal the way personal attachment histories, or early relationships with caregivers may be fraught with abandonment, abuse, neglect, harshness, and other unloving behaviors; however, through the muck and mire, though they start out as tragic stories fraught with pain, hope is not lost. There are both clinical and spiritual interventions (and in some cases both) that can help people like Grace work to resolve loss and make sense of her story, bringing beauty from ashes. Irving Yalom, who is a prolific writer in the area of psychotherapy has identified a number of therapeutic factors that therapists are encouraged to use. One of these is called, "the instillation of hope", which is said to bring clients a sense of optimism. The idea that a person's history does not determine their destiny, and that there is hope for a brighter future, is both one of our tasks as therapists for instilling in our clients. It is also, from a biblical perspective, something that is important to remind ourselves us as we seek to renew our minds. Isaiah 61:1-3 (ISV) clearly articulates the promise of hope and restoration:

> "to provide for those who grieve in Zion—to bestow on them a crown of beauty instead of ashes, the oil of gladness instead of mourning, a mantle of praise instead of a spirit of despair. Then people will call them 'Oaks of Righteousness', 'The Planting of the Lord', in order to display his splendor."

One of my stellar students, who we'll call Arnold for the purposes of confidentiality, has overcome and thrived in the face of adversity, has helped me see how the above quote by Helen Keller and the Lotus flower depicted here could represent the process of overcoming challenges in an inspiring way. Similar to a beautiful Lotus flower stretching up towards heaven despite the muck all around it, it emerges beautiful, strong, clear, bright, pure, resilient, and lovely. Grace's relationship with her grandmother was an example of a secure autonomous relationship. The loss of that relationship and other attachment related injuries could put Grace on a trajectory towards an unresolved or disorganized attachment style. Thus, the purpose of this book is to reveal important attachment dynamics that influence the stories of our clients, students, and supervisees and to highlight the dynamics in such a way to facilitate empathy. A second purpose of this book is to go beyond facilitating empathy and understanding but to also share research based strategies that can facilitate healing from depression and attachment injuries as well as spiritual strategies that help our clients connect with the author and finisher of their faith who has a hope and a future in store with the best yet to come. The following pages are designed to serve as a guidebook for those in the helping professions (specifically Clinical Mental Health Counselors and Pastoral Counselors) wanting an attachment informed perspective and interventions that are clinically and spiritually relevant. People who have a secure attachment style tend to have better peer relationships and better adult love relationships according to attachment experts (Marvin, 2013); therefore, as clinicians we want to help our clients move in this direction.

Let's look at how the dynamics of Grace's story may fit with some of the attachment related dynamics that will unfold with the pages of this book. The phrase (Tennyson, 1850), "it is better to have loved and lost than to never have loved at all" is the mantra of the secure autonomous attachment style (Sibcy, 2015, personal communication). On a gold standard assessment called, "The Adult Attachment Interview" or AAI for short; (we will talk more about this later in *Chapter 3: Measuring your attachment style*), an attachment classification is provided, in association with a person's interview, thus revealing a secure, preoccupied, avoidant, or unresolved attachment style (Main & Goldwyn, 1980). We will talk about each of these attachment styles and what they entail in the next chapter. Two important characteristics of a secure autonomous attachment style are coherence and valuing. Grace's narrative both indicated how she valued her grandmother (notice it was indicated that Grace misses her grandmother, cherishes the memories, and honored her grandmother's request). Also, based on the way Grace shared her story with us, it was apparent that her memories of her attachment relationship with her grandmother (despite being decades old) were also very coherent painting a clear picture of what the relationship was like. Can you imagine Grace snuggled up next to her grandmother reading a book, Grace's brown eyes winkling as she is gazing up at her grandmother in awe with her cheeks surrounded by her auburn hair? Can you imagine her grandmother's warmth as she comforted Grace in her kind and gentle voice? Grace used the adjective "loving" to describe her relationship with her Grandmother, and described a scenario where they were snuggled up reading a book as well as her Grandmother preparing her for the future, for the loss of a highly valued relationship, and introducing her to a Savior: all clear evidence to support the adjective, "loving." Grace's grandmother introduced her to the Savior and revealed the idea that Christ will never leave or forsake her. It is as if she was preparing Grace for her death and priming her to be open to receive comfort from her Heavenly Father. This is reminiscent of what Jesus did with his disciples: he prepared them for his departure and also let them know that He would not leave them alone. He left them with the Comforter. Jesus said to his disciples before his departure to Heaven (John 14:15–18, ISV),

> "'If you love me, keep my commandments. I will ask the Father to give you another Helper, to be with you always. He is the Spirit of truth, whom the world cannot receive, because it neither sees him nor recognizes him. But you recognize him, because he lives with you and will be in you. I'm not going to forsake you like orphans. I will come back to you.'"

CHAPTER 1 SUMMARY

The Adult Attachment Interview, or AAI for short, is an assessment that helps us determine what a person's attachment style is. The result of this psychological assessment is that it classifies a person's attachment style in one of four categories: secure, preoccupied, avoidant, or unresolved. In this chapter, the story of Grace and her relationship to her grandmother illustrates an example of the secure autonomous relationship. This attachment style has two important characteristics, that of coherence and valuing. Grace used the adjective "loving" to describe her relationship with her Grandmother, and described a scenario where they were snuggled up reading a book, and her Grandmother was preparing her for the future, for the loss of the highly valued relationship (that was clearly important to both of them), and introducing her to a Savior and comforter, clear evidence to support that adjective, "loving." Clear and coherent memories and an attachment story that is recounted in a consistent way is an important part of the process of making sense of one's history and one of the indicator of a movement towards a secure attachment style. The story of Grace gives us an idea of what these attachment stories can be like, reminds us of the importance and role that God, our ultimate attachment figure can serve, and sets the stage for us to talk about the nature of the specifics of attachment relationships in more detail in the next chapter.

CHAPTER 2
Attachment Styles and Relationship Dynamics

"We long for an affection altogether ignorant of our faults. Heaven has accorded this to us in the uncritical canine attachment."

—*George Eliot*

In the introductory quote, George Eliot highlights the longing that we have for an unconditional love or acceptance, and how a dog and his or her human may experience this, due in large part to the nature of the canine. After all, how would you describe a puppy after spending some time feeding, walking, and providing it with affection? Loyal, forgiving (still comes to you after you leave him home alone all day while you are at work), affectionate (lots of licks and proximity seeking), and happy to see you always! Every day when I come home from work, it is like my two toy poodles (Sandy and Brandon) are throwing me a party complete with singing and dancing. They have been trained as therapy dogs, one embraces the role and the other is not so fond of socializing with others, but when I come home Sandy throws back her little head (they are seven pound dogs) and lets out a great big howl (of course I tell her that she sings beautifully), and Brandon runs around in a circle doing a little happy dance. Dogs are attached and seek proximity to their attachment figures. Dogs can teach us a lot about the nature of attachment. According to Dr. Thomas Lee, people who have dogs may even live longer (however this may be due to the walking and activity that they require) rather than the attachment (Harvard Health Blog, 2015).

If you are not as familiar with clinical language, you may be wondering what the term attachment means and what it involves. Let's take a moment to unpack the concept. John Bowlby (1969) has been referred to as the Father of Attachment. His development of attachment theory was influenced by a number of related fields including developmental psychology and ethology. In recent years, Bowlby's original work has also been extended and informed by "interpersonal neurobiology" (Cassidy, 1994; Siegel, 1999, & Siegel, 2001). Attachment experiences serve to inform the attachment behavioral system which serves as a major role in life processes. The attachment behavioral system is part of the neurobiological foundation for emotion regulation and also the development of self-other relationship rules (or schemas), and the attachment behavioral system also regulates the capacity for balancing both autonomy and intimacy (Sibcy & Knight, 2017). Bowlby (1982) described attachment as involving a tendency for a child to seek closeness to a caregiver or other person who is perceived as better able to manage the crudeness of reality. The attachment behavioral system is activated when a child feels threatened and then seeks proximity to a caregiver for comfort, which is often the child's safe haven. Once the child feels comforted, he or she is able to move from this "secure base" back out into the world to explore the environment, perhaps using monitoring glances to check back with the caregiver to make sure they are still accessible and in close proximity. John Bowlby's research partner Mary Salter Ainsworth worked with him on many projects (More specifically, she was described as "John Bowlby's partner in research for more than 40 years" by Steel and Steele (2016, p. 277). Later Mary Ainsworth had Bob Marvin as a student (therefore he is a direct academic descendant of Bowlby) and Bob Marvin has continued the research by developing explanatory models and teaching on attachment in what he calls the "Circle of Security" (Marvin, 2016, personal communication, Liberty University) in which he illustrates this cycle with a circle. When a group of college professors asked Dr. Bob Marvin, "If there was one thing you wanted all counselors and counseling students to know about attachment, what would it be?" Dr. Marvin paused for a moment and contemplated the question. Then, he thoughtfully responded with enthusiasm, "I would like for them all to see the concept illustrated in the following comic, 'Rose' that illustrates the concept of attachment in a nutshell" (Brady, 2002; Marvin & Seagroves, 2017). For more information on Dr. Marvin's materials, please see the list of recommended readings at the end of this book. *The comic displays the idea that we get depleted for various reasons, and we need to recharge. This can happen through a loving, affectionate embrace, and then once we feel comforted and sufficiently snuggled, we are ready to go out and explore the world fully charged.*

Bowlby used a thermostat as a metaphor for the attachment behavioral system. *Bowlby illustrated that the child is not necessarily seeking an object (the mother or father). Rather, the child is seeking to maintain a safe distance from that attachment figure consistently.*

So, who is an attachment figure? The first attachment figure is typically the mother or primary caregiver. Other attachment figures may include: parents, grandparents, step-parents, babysitters or other caretakers. The key is (based on the work of Mary Ainsworth) a person has to meet four basic criteria to serve as an attachment figure. First, they have to be a safe haven, a place that the child can go to seek comfort during times of distress. For example, when a child falls and bumps his knee he may return to his mother in tears, perhaps she says (as my mother did), "Let me kiss it and make it better." The child is soon after comforted and returns to play.

Secondly, the attachment figure needs to serve as a secure base. This can be considered like a launching pad. Think of a plane as it leaves the airport runway and has advanced navigational systems and technologies that allow it to stay in connection with the airport. Whenever things are going well, and the plane is fully resourced and operational, the pilot takes it out to navigate the skies. If there is a problem, the pilot keeps the plane stationed at the airport/the secure base until things are resolved or recharged to the extent that it is safe for the plan to go out and "explore" the skies!

The third requirement for an attachment figure is that they need to be available so that the child can seek closeness to them. For example, the child may see a stranger enter the room and then go hide behind the mother until she feels comfortable that the stranger is safe.

The final requirement for the attachment figure is that there be a sense of distress when there is a separation or loss. For example, Belinda took her two-year-old daughter Bella to the nursery for Sunday school so she could attend the church service When Bella could see that her mother was heading for the door without her, Bella let out shrieks and cries at the top of her lungs. Belinda quickly stepped outside the door and quietly waited behind the closed door, listening to Bella crying at the top of her lungs and protesting her departure. This is an example of the distress that can happen during times of separation in an attachment relationship. The way the attachment figure fulfills these roles and the nature of their availability and the bond between them is associated with several different styles of attachment.

When I was training to learn how to code the Adult Attachment Interview (AAI), to uncover client's attachment style and use this content for therapeutic and research purposes, I met an interesting colleague from Switzerland. She shared that she was trained as an attorney but partnered with her husband who was a psychotherapist. She had been doing Adult Attachment Interviews for many years. When working with clients, she would do a session and interview the client with the AAI, then send the recorded interview off to be transcribed, and would then code the results and write up a brief report (quite a labor intensive process, but very helpful for the client's therapeutic journey). She would then join her husband in therapy to reveal the results to the client in the form of a short report. Subsequently, her husband (the psychotherapist) would work with the client for a given number of counseling sessions, and afterwards would do a re-test/second interview and compare results to see if the client had improved. My colleague returned to AAI training after ten years of doing this coding because she shared lately that all of the transcripts she coded were illustrating the same attachment classification, unresolved. She wanted to make sure she was correct and was not starting to see all unresolved cases through a clouded lens.

From her ten years of coding the AAI and seeing therapeutic progress towards secure attachment she shared with me what she noticed about those who tend to speak with a coherent narrative (and manifest a secure attachment style). This resonated with me, and I never forgot it, so I would like to share it with you.

This veteran Adult Attachment Interview coder shared that the distinguishing factor between a secure and an insecure attachment story was that, for a secure person, speaking about their attachment style in the interview, had an experience where someone taught them what love is. She indicated that in some *ways transcripts (word for word write up for the AAI/attachment story) of those with a more preoccupied or avoidant style reveal a surprising commonality, a common unknown ... no one has taught them what love is.* Grace's Grandmother taught her, years ago, what love is, and this laid the foundation for a secure autonomous attachment style (later we will discuss whether this was a continuous secure attachment style or a earned secure attachment style illustrated in Grace's case).

We have discussed the secure autonomous attachment style as an adaptive attachment style that can develop when things go well and when a child has a responsive primary caregiver (whether that is a biological parent, grandparent, stepparent, or other caregiver). I like the way it has been explained in the text "*Why You Do the Things You Do: The Secret to Healthy Relationships*" by Clinton and Sibcy. The authors discuss the idea that attachment is another term that can be synonymous with relationship and relationships are governed by relationship rules (Clinton & Sibcy, 2006). *If one believes that he is worthy of love and others are capable of loving him then typically a secure autonomous attachment style emerges.* On the other hand, if the answer to one of those relationship questions ("Am I worthy of love?" and "Are others able to show me love?") is "No," then an insecure or disorganized attachment relationship may develop. Let's explore what the three attachment styles look like in simplistic terms and then in more detail in the next section.

ATTACHMENT STYLES

"Piglet sidled up to Pooh from behind. 'Pooh!' he whispered.

'Yes, Piglet?' 'Nothing' said Piglet, taking Pooh's paw, 'I just wanted to be sure of you.'"

© catwalker/Shutterstock.com

 As the quote above suggests, part of the attachment process involves what Piglet refers to as "being sure of" which may involve some degree of anxiety and/or avoidance. *The security of the attachment and the style that develops may be a function of how sure we are of the reliability of our attachment relationships.* There are a few different styles that manifest and different authors and researchers describe these styles in different ways. I will share with you some conceptualizations I have found most helpful and where they emerged.

My colleague, mentor, and Attachment Guru, Dr. Gary Sibcy introduced me to an Adult Attachment Interview coder named Dean Dozier. I was fascinated by Dean's experience coding AAIs and excited to hear insights from someone who was so experienced. I had an opportunity to talk with Dean about her work on a visit I made up to Afton Mountain to see her. She is a nature photographer and AAI coder. She has coded thousands of AAI transcripts for eating disorder facilities, hospitals, private practices, and for research purposes (As a side note: I recommend her as a coder, for more information on coding and her contact information see Appendix A). I asked her what she had learned about distinguishing tough cases (for example, whether an AAI transcript was secure with some dismissing tendencies or dismissing with some secure tendencies), and she said she noticed that people tend to be oriented in one primary direction moving towards the discussion, moving away from it, or getting tangled up in it. I like this approach to describing attachment style in a nutshell:

Secure = comfortable moving towards a discussion on attachment

Dismissing = moving away from discussing attachment

Preoccupied = getting all tangled up in a discussion of attachment

Unresolved = incongruent accounts of loss or abuse

From reviewing many transcripts, doing clinical work, supervision, and studying attachment for the past 15 years, I have observed some distinguishing features of each style and how attachment orientations manifest. Let's take a look at each attachment style and what these tendencies may look like in various cases.

The Dismissing Style

A dismissing attachment style is one that many Adult Attachment Interview Coders may enjoy, sometimes almost as much as the vivid, coherent, clear recounting of a secure attachment history. This is because they are usually very easy to complete because of their brevity. From my experience, they tend to be a bit on the shorter side (no sweeping generalizations can be concluded, but this is based on anecdotal experience).

A client named Shakespeare (name changed for the purposes of confidentiality) responded with some dismissing tendencies. In session I asked Shakespeare, "You mentioned that your relationship with your father was 'loving.' Would you share a specific memory that illustrates what lead you to select the term 'loving' to describe your childhood relationship with your father?"

Shakespeare responded, "Hmm . . . I cannot think of anything right now."

I replied, "Take all the time you need, there is no rush" (this was not an official AAI). Shakespeare looked very concerned as his neutral eyebrows furrowed and the corners of his mouth quickly turned downward into a frown, without pause, he emphatically said, "We could be here all day long!"

I gently responded, "Okay we'll take just another minute then." Shakespeare looked very uncomfortable, and I looked away to give him a minute, and he very quickly told me, "I just can't think of anything right now." Shakespeare was a classic example of one with a dismissing attachment style. He was turning away from the discussion of attachment. The thought of taking time to think about an attachment oriented memory that represented how his relationship with his father was loving was extremely uncomfortable. It is not clear from the research whether one with a dismissing style is consciously idealizing the attachment relationship and wanting to preserve the belief, for instance in Shakespeare's case that his relationship with his father was loving, despite a dearth of evidence or what the internal process is of the dismissing speaker. However, the mantra of the dismissing style may be said to be, "Why open yourself up to love, when it hurts so darn much when it doesn't work out. Just avoid the disappointment."

Some assessments and researchers categorize attachment styles based on attachment related avoidance or attachment related anxiety (Regarding a popular scale that measures these two dimensions, the Experiences in Close Relationships Scale, specifically it has been stated, "The Experiences in Close Relationships Scale (ECR) developed by Brennan and colleagues (1998), has been widely used and many studies have supported its validity. As you can see, the dismissing attachment style tends to be characterized by attachment related avoidance, in other words, a turning away from the discussion of attachment. The prototypical dismissing speaker would tend to be low on attachment related anxiety" (Cassidy & Shaver, 2016).

At first glance, it may seem hard to be empathic towards the tough outer shell of one with a dismissing attachment style. However, the literature reveals some interesting findings regarding the dismissing style. As early as three years of age, researchers found that these children had learned to mask their emotions. You see, the child with a dismissing attachment relationship has a very challenging task. The child has to maintain proximity to a rejecting caregiver. If the child protests rejection too much, then they risk alienating the caregiver entirely. Hence, the turning away from the attachment figures in this situation may turn out to be adaptive. In research, looking at children's behavior in the strange situation when their parents left them in a nursery with a stranger, many of the children cried and protested and had spikes in physiological markers of arousal such as heightened cortisol responses and heightened heart rate associated with their crying and other outbursts. On the other hand, the dismissing child did not exhibit much outward protest behavior at all. It appeared they were unscathed by the departure of their caretaker. However, upon a closer look, it was revealed that they were experiencing the same physiological stress as the children with the other attachment styles. Therefore, before they were even toddlers, they had already learned how to mask their distress.

The Preoccupied Style

The individual with a preoccupied attachment style tends to be opposite the one with the avoidant or dismissing attachment style in many ways. Preoccupation tends to be associated with high levels of anxiety and low levels of avoidance.

Let's look at the case of Shenequa.

Shenequa came to couples counseling with her boyfriend, Jack. They were an attractive young couple. Shenequa was very in love with Jack and was willing to give up most of her priorities or distinctive opinions in order to maintain her relationship with him. Jack reported feeling smothered by Shenequa and wanting more space. He shared when he went into his garage to work in his wood shop he wanted to be alone, and he mentioned Shenequa would always come in to ask him how it was going. Shenequa wanted more contact but said she would give that up in order to maintain her relationship with Jack. Shenequa thought about Jack all the time, but she did not understand why Jack was not more available. During their dating relationship, Jack came down with a horrible flu. He was very sick and really wanted to be alone with the commode. He apologized to Shenequa for having to cancel their date, but explained he had been throwing up and experiencing many other symptoms of the flu and did not want to get her sick. Shenequa was desperate to see Jack, and she could not bear to be apart from him another night that she did not even think about his request to have time alone to recover. Shenequa thought she would stop and pick up Jack some soup and have a perfect excuse to come and see him! Jack was exasperated and had the sense that Shenequa did not respect his wishes. Shenequa could not believe that Jack would not want her to be there. Shenequa was talking with her friend Cheyenne. Cheyenne wanted to tell Shenequa about a recent hobby she had taken up but Shenequa kept changing the topic of conversation back to Jack. It was like she had a one track mind and wanted Cheyenne to help her analyze the relationship. She was high in anxiety and wanted to get things right to make sure that the relationship worked. Shenequa struggled to regulate her thoughts and redirect them away from the relationship. Her anxiety about her relationship with Jack made it difficult to focus on other things and she often found her thoughts preoccupying.

The Continuous Secure Style

The continuous secure attachment style, or prototypical secure attachment style, is typically manifested in a person with low levels of attachment avoidance and low levels of anxiety. They are able to talk freely about their attachment experiences, tend to value attachment figures, and tend to be forgiving and collaborative when speaking with others about their attachments.

Let's look at a client named Sally. Sally grew up in Long Island and had a strong personality. Sally loved people and especially loved her family. Sally shared that she was experiencing some stress balancing work and life. Sally shared, "My daughter Jessica is getting ready to graduate high school. Can you believe it? Aww, my dear sweet Jessie finishing high school, and she has a dear boyfriend, Jordan! Aww, Jordan is so wonderful! They started a band together and have been playing love songs. Jessie on vocals and Jordan on the piano, and they fill my home with music! I am going to miss my dear ones so much! My Dad would be so proud! You know when my Dad was alive, he filled our house with songs. We would make veggie shakes in the blender and sing old Jewish songs together every Saturday morning! He was really into health and running and so am I, and so we did that together! Aww, I miss Pappi! I wish my Pappi could have lived to see Jessie all grown up!" Can you picture Sally in her kitchen with her Pappi making a veggie shake and singing? She often presents vivid pictures of her attachment experiences with a sense of clarity and congruence, and she always seems to attach a high value to her attachment experiences.

EARNED SECURE

Recall, in the opening chapter we discussed "The Case for Grace" and we found that Grace had loving experiences with her Grandmother. She valued the relationship, she missed her grandmother dearly after she passed away, she still remembers her Grandmother fondly, and she values all that her Grandmother taught her. These are all characteristics of a secure autonomous speaker's transcript or attachment story. However, despite her loving experiences with her Grandmother, Grace also had to come to terms with the loss of an attachment figure.

After Grace's Grandmother passed away, Grace went through a period of grieving. Grace describes it this way, "My heart was broken with grief and I did not have words for it. I remember when I found out, a friend of the family told me, and I sat frozen for a moment. Then I went to my room and held my teddy bear and cried. That teddy bear reminded me that Jesus was with me and somehow that made me feel close to Grandmother, knowing that she was in Heaven with Jesus and I could experience his Spirit comforting me. Back then, I was very young, and I did not really have words to describe what was happening, but I knew the idea of Heaven and Jesus was comforting in light of one of my young life's greatest heartbreaks." Grace mentioned she felt like a part of her died when her grandmother died. At this point, some people develop an unresolved attachment style because they have a difficult time coming to terms internally with an external change. Grace went on to experience a barrage of psychological insults in experiences with other early caregivers; however, she maintained a valuing, forgiving, and coherent style with the capacity to discuss these negative experiences without having to deny, repress, hide or otherwise twist her narrative in an incoherent way. Thus, to be more specific, Grace has secure tendencies, but depending on her recounting of her perceived childhood experiences and how loving or unloving they were, her AAI may reveal a classification of Earned Secure. We will talk more about the Earned Secure Classification in Chapter 6.

Unresolved for Loss (or Trauma)

Bowlby, the Father of Classical Attachment Theory, discussed the concept that losing an attachment figure is disorganizing in and of itself, and requires a person to make an internal shift to account for the external shift that has happened. If a person gets stuck on the loss, and has not come to terms with it, then they are said to have an "unresolved attachment status." Here is an example from a client I worked with named Orris (name has been changed for confidentiality purposes). Orris' wife of over 40 years passed away after he cared for her for several years due to debilitating diabetes where she had one leg amputated and was unable to walk. When discussing the loss, through heaving sobs, Orris said, "It was horrible. I had to watch her go through tremendous suffering . . ." He went on to share, "We liked to attend church together and work on our garden together, so I spend a lot of time working on my garden. We are gardeners at heart and we are the kind of people that would much rather be in the garden than at the beach." Notice that Orris is still responding to the situation talking about his relationship with his wife as if she is living. He describes himself as a part of the "we" but the conversation was taking place about six months after her death. At this point in time, he had not yet completely made that internal shift and resolved the loss. If he continues talking about her in the present as if she is still living, but died six months ago and acknowledges that, then I would describe this as an incongruent account of the loss. Researchers using the Adult Attachment Interview would look for language like this and highly trained coders would determine whether the account of the loss was incoherent enough for Orris to have an unresolved attachment classification. Orris also uses language that indicates he really valued his relationship with his wife, so it is possible that his secondary attachment classification would be secure. An AAI would provide a more complete picture of Orris' attachment story.

CHAPTER 2 SUMMARY

Based on discussions with some veteran Adult Attachment Interview coders, who have analyzed many AAI transcripts, a surprising theme emerged. A commonality between the attachment styles is that they all revolve around how someone is taught what love is. Those who tend to speak with a coherent narrative (and manifest a secure autonomous attachment style) display a distinguishing factor, namely, that someone taught them what love is while those with a preoccupied or avoidant attachment style indicate the opposite.

How one answers the questions "Am I worthy of love?" and "Are others able to show me love?" are key distinctions. Someone with a secure autonomous attachment style believes that he is worthy of love and that others are capable of loving them. If the answer to those questions ("Am I worthy of love? "Are others competent to show me love?") is "No," then an insecure or disorganized attachment relationship may develop. According to Bowlby, the Father of Classical Attachment Theory, losing an attachment figure is a disorganizing situation and requires a person to account for this external shift by making an internal shift. If they become stuck on the loss and have not resolved the loss internally, they are said to have an "unresolved attachment status".

However, hope is not lost. A fifth style has emerged in attachment research. The Earned Secure Attachment, may develop when one has experiences that would lead to an insecure attachment but instead a person maintains a valuing, forgiving and coherent style without having to deny, repress, hide, or otherwise twist the narrative of their attachment story in an incoherent way.

Researchers and highly trained coders who use the Adult Attachment Interview look for language that help them determine the classification for each type. In the next chapter, we will explore how the AAI can be a valuable tool to use in clinical work with clients, and why we use it in our clinical work whenever possible and encourage others to use it as well. We also encourage clients to ask their therapists for an Adult Attachment Interview and report.

CHAPTER 3

Measuring Your Attachment Style: The Gold Standard

"The measure of who we are is what we do with what we have."

— *Vince Lombardi*

Now that you've been reading about attachment you may be wondering what your attachment or relationship style is. Psychologists and counselors use various tests to measure personality, mood, and many other characteristics. We call these tests "assessments", but we will use the term "test" here to simplify things moving forward.

One popular test that measures attachment is called the Adult Attachment Interview, or AAI for short. The AAI was created by three colleagues, Carol George, Nancy Kaplan, and Mary Main in 1985. The AAI is a semi-structured interview that lasts about an hour depending on the state of mind of the participant (preoccupied speakers tend to have longer interviews, and transcripts, while dismissing speakers tend to have shorter interviews/ transcripts). The hallmark question of the AAI is, "Would you share with me five adjectives to describe your childhood relationship with your mother?" (George, Kaplan, & Main, 1985 as cited in AAI protocol: http://www.psychology.sunysb.edu/attachment/measures/content/aai_interview.pdf;). The protocol to the Adult Attachment interview has been made available online to help consumers of the research understand the protocol. You can download it at the following web address (as of September 13, 2017): http://www.psychology.sunysb.edu/attachment/measures/content/aai_interview.pdf. After requesting the five adjectives, the interviewer then jots down the five adjectives the speaker uses and then the interviewer surprises the speaker's unconscious with the next questions on the AAI asking them to give support for previous answers, see the AAI protocol to see what the questions are (the link is provide above). Later in the interview, speakers are asked about their childhood experiences related to feeling rejected, and the reasons they thought their parents acted the way they did. Here were a series of other questions asked and one of the latter questions was, "How did your experiences influence your adult personality?" (Main, Kaplan, & Cassidy, 1985, p. 90). Main, Kaplan, and Cassidy discuss in a very prominent chapter entitled "Security in Infancy, Childhood, and Adulthood: A Move to the Level of Representation" published in the 1985 edition of "Monographs of the Society for Research in Child Development," that the parents in their study that completed the AAI and were found to have a secure attachment had some features in common.

Let's take a look at those common features of secure autonomous parents. These secure parents were found to value attachment relationships. Interestingly, not only did they tend to value attachment relationships and consider them influential, but they were also able to recall them with some level of objectivity. However, Main, Kaplan, Cassidy, and Goldwyn also reported that "Many had unfavorable attachment relationships in childhood, particularly in the form of loss or rejection" (Main & Goldwyn, in press as cited in Main, Kaplan, & Cassidy, 1985, p. 91).

In early research on the AAI and infant strange situation (please note, the strange situation is an experiment that Mary Ainsworth and Bowlby worked on, along with many other attachment researchers that followed them, that examined what children would do when their mother left for a few minutes and they were in a nursery with a stranger, they examined again what they would do at reunion, when their mother returned). Research has also reported that secure speakers, in addition to valuing attachment and indicating that they perceived attachment experiences as having a role in influencing their development, and remaining objective in descriptions of experiences with caregivers, they also noticed a few other characteristics of secure speakers. One was a "readiness of recall" (Main, Kaplan, & Cassidy, 1985, p. 91), and the second other prominent characteristic of the secure speaker was that they tended to demonstrate a tendency "in discussing attachment that suggested much reflection prior to the interview and a lack of idealization of parents or of past experiences" (Main, Kaplan, & Cassidy, 1985, p. 91). I would like to share with you a passage that Mary Main and her colleagues Kaplan and Cassidy found in the transcripts of a parent of a securely attached son because I think it is a vivid description of the redemptive nature of the earned secure attachment style (where a person can have any number of various difficult or painful childhood experience, and still develop a secure autonomous attachment style; Main, Kaplan, Cassidy, 1985, p. 91).

> "When asked about early relationships, one man rated as secure began with 'You've struck a goldmine, actually . . .' and launched on a history of rejection, loss, abuse, and major separations. His interview responses indicated much prior reflection. When asked the question, 'Was there ever a time in childhood where you felt rejected?' this father of a secure son laughed heartily: 'If *that* ain't rejection I don't know what the hell is!'"

It sounds like this gentleman was able to discuss his past attachment experiences in a coherent and somewhat objective way, acknowledging the difficulty and the pain without idealizing. As the authors shared above, this indicated that he spent some time (before the interview) at some point reflecting and taking time to make sense of his experiences. This is an interesting capacity in story-telling (more about this later in the text). Based on these descriptions from the peer-reviewed research (Main, Kaplan, & Cassidy, 1985), we see that those who share the story of their attachment history (in interview format of the AAI) in a secure way tend to talk about how their attachment relationships are important to them or signify in some way that they value and prize those relationships. At the same time, in addition to having positive experiences, many secure speakers also had difficult experiences associated with loss of attachment figures or rejection associated with attachment figures. Their story was still characterized by valuing attachment, but they were able to talk about their experiences in an objective way (whether positive or negative). We will talk more about this important capacity in the storytelling chapter.

When speakers, during the AAI, tell their story in a clear way, this helps the coder (note, there is a rigorous certification process coders must go through before being certified by Mary Main as a reliable coder. I recommend this if you are interested in using the assessment in clinical practice regularly, and especially if you would like to learn more about how it is coded, see more below. You can also administer the interview and have someone else code it, see appendix B with the contact information of Dean Dozier, who is a certified reliable coder of the AAI who has many experienced coders, as well as some other certified reliable coders) to identify their strong coherence. The AAI will allow you to uncover information that reveals the speaker's state of mind with respect to their early attachment relationships.

The Adult Attachment Interview (AAI) protocol and the unpublished manuscript or manual that coders use to analyze the AAI transcript (the transcription of the interview) is only available to trained coders who participate in a two-week training as part of the process to become certified as a trained and reliable coder. This process is rigorous and has been affectionately referred to as "AAI Boot Camp" (Sroufe, personal communication, 2014) and is followed by a testing period. However, if you want to use AAI's regularly in practice and are interested in learning to code, I highly recommend it. Dan Siegel, a well-respected speaker on the topic of mental health known for defining terms like "mental health" and speaking and publishing on the topic of neuroscience is a proponent of the AAI. At a conference sponsored by Harvard Medical School and McLean Hospital (Siegel, 2012, personal communication), I spoke with Siegel after his presentation about the AAI. I told him about our interest in the assessment and the training we were involved in. Dr. Siegel shared that he had also been trained in the AAI as well (this is a significant time commitment, so this speaks to his respect and valuing of this as a test and clinical tool).

In clinical (meaning settings where the AAI is used as a part of the assessment or treatment of mental health disorders; or as a therapeutic tool) use of the AAI has been described as "deep" which has been defined as a tool that reflects "both early memories and modes of responding to (or coping with) experience stored at diverse levels of awareness" (Steele and Baradon, 2004, p. 287). Each speaker is assessed in terms of the nature of their childhood experiences, their state of mind with respect to their caregivers, and experiences related to the loss of early attachment figures (including grandparents) and abuse or traumatic experiences with that involved any early attachment figures.

Clinicians, psychologists, and clinical mental health counselors, also known as Licensed Professional Counselors (LPC's), who advocate for the use of the AAI in treatment argue that using this protocol of questions may prompt the revelation of abuse and other experiences earlier in the therapeutic process. Another benefit to using the AAI in treatment is that it facilitates the exploration of both emotional and cognitive domains that may be challenging and prompts the speaker, or client in this case, to integrate the content (Steele and Baradon, 2004).

Howard Steel and Miriam Steel, at the New School in New York City, edited a book called, *Clinical Applications of the AAI*, published by Guilford Press in March of 2008. In their text, they discuss some of the benefits of using the AAI such as the AAI "can help establish a therapeutic alliance, facilitate shared goals for therapeutic work, and serve as a source of understanding and motivation that facilitate the therapeutic processes measurement of progress and outcome" (Steel & Steel, 2008, p. 30). They share that *one of the reasons the AAI has garnered the widespread attention it has is because of the way it reveals a central and important idea, which is the "ability or lack thereof, to show an organized credible and consistent valuing of attachment relationships" (Steel & Steel, 2008, p. 30).*

ANOTHER MEASURE: THE EXPERIENCES IN CLOSE RELATIONSHIPS SCALE

Although we recommend using the AAI whenever possible such as for starting therapy (Main & Hess, 2000) or for measurement or research purposes, we recognize that sometimes this may not be feasible due to environmental constraints. Another popular instrument used to assess dimensions of adolescent or adult attachment (romantic, rather than parent child) is the Experiences in Close Relationships-revised or the Experiences in Close Relationships Structure Scale (ECR; ECR-RS; Fraley, Heffernan, Vicary, & Brumbaugh, 2011). It is a questionnaire that measures two different dimensions of attachment: relationship anxiety and relationship avoidance (Sibley, Fisher, & Liu, 2005). Researchers indicate that the ECR is a "widely used instrument" (Pedersen, Eikenæs, Urnes, Skulberg, & Wilberg, 2015, p. 208). The ECR-RS version has extended the original assessment from measures of romantic attachment to also look at parental and best friend domains of attachment in 15–18-year-olds (validated on non-clinical samples of adolescents; Feddern & Elklit, 2014). Researchers report that the ECR and the ECR-R are "currently the most valid and most commonly used measures of adult attachment" (Donabek & Elkit, 2014, p. 60). In our research, we like using the AAI because of the richness and depth that emerges from a person's narrative, subsequent attachment classification that is determined after a tedious and detail oriented coding process. The scales such as coherence also allow for quantitative measures of improvement for research purposes or measures of clinical improvement. However, when not possible due to financial or time limitations, we have also found the ECR useful in our clinical work and research.

RESULTS

Once we conduct an Adult Attachment Interview you may be wondering, "What do these attachment styles look like in the interview?" Each one has distinct characteristics (Main, Kaplan, & Cassidy, 1985). It is important to note that the coding process classifies the transcript based on many factors such as coherence of transcript (one area we look for to target for improvement in our clinical work), coherence of mind, idealization, etc. that leads (along with many other factors) to a final attachment classification.

Coders go through a very complex analysis process that involves much study and careful analysis and training in the two-week AAI coding course. For more information on training opportunities in the AAI, please see the following website (as of September, 2017, the cost on the website is listed as $1,700 plus a $600 reliability testing course): http://www.psychology.sunysb.edu/attachment/AAI_training/aai_training_statement.htm

It is worth noting that speakers, in the Adult Attachment Interview, do not have to have a perfect childhood or perfectly loving parents in order to have a classification of secure. Rather, they have to have "made sense of their experiences" as Siegel would say (Siegel, 2009, 0.01). Siegel discusses that the research shows if a person does the hard work of "making sense" of their life, then they can create change in structure or function in the brain, which leads to neural integration and a more resilient life.

In other words, the discussion needs to be considered coherent. The speaker needs to stay on topic, have evidence for what he or she says, be concise, and yet sufficiently answer the questions without considerable grammatical slips or slips into exaggerative speech or passive speech.

This looks different with each attachment style. The preoccupied speaker tends to have a relatively longer transcript than that of dismissing or secure speakers. Typically their discussion of attachment figures is not concise and/or it may also be incomplete. For example, rather than answering a question directly, succinctly, and completely when describing a memory that illustrates why they chose the adjective "complicated" to describe their childhood relationship with their mother, they may begin discussing the phone conversation they had with her yesterday (even though they were asked about the relationship during early childhood).

Secure autonomous transcriptions, unlike the previous two attachment styles discussed, tend to be succinct, complete, relevant, fresh, and make sense. This reminds me of Siegel's description of "making sense" being one of the most important requirements for moving towards a Secure Autonomous status. Perhaps one could speculate that the prototypical Secure Autonomous speakers may have had a loving childhood and fewer difficult experiences to make sense of, unlike a speaker whose childhood was plagued with felt rejection and unloving behaviors. It may be quite challenging for a speaker who experiences rejection combined with loving behaviors from parents to state that their parents were unloving without idealizing them (similar to those with an avoidant or dismissing stance), blaming them (similar to a preoccupied orientation), or making incongruent statements like acknowledging abuse and renouncing that abuse occurred (a more disorganized approach). It seems, perhaps it is more difficult to acknowledge unloving behavior by calling it what it is with congruent description and then forgive the behavior.

This is also reminiscent of the challenge of emotional intelligence which involves being open to emotions both positive and negative—without exaggerating the positive or minimizing the negative. An emotionally intelligent person is thought to have access to both positive and negative emotions, and to be able to harness them to meet intended goals. Salovey and Grewal (2005) in their article entitled, "The Science of Emotional Intelligence" published in "Current Directions in Psychological Science" a publication of the American Psychological Association, discuss how a politician, if he or she has high levels of emotional intelligence, may take his anger and harness it to help him deliver a powerful speech that can evoke emotion in the listeners, such as righteous anger. Salovey and Grewal (2005, p. 282) conclude, "Therefore the emotionally intelligent person can harness emotions, even negative ones, and manage them to achieve intended goals." A client wanting to overcome adverse attachment experience and move towards a secure attachment style may benefit from harnessing the emotions of hope and compassion and use these emotions to put on new lenses for examining his or her attachment story.

It can be painful and uncomfortable to feel negative emotions, and one of the great motivations in life is not the pursuit of pleasure but the avoidance of pain. Oftentimes a number of coping mechanisms are used to avoid pain or to reduce the intensity of that pain such as self-preservation, distraction, and optimism (Pichurin, 2017).

Children often seek to cope with distress by engaging their caregivers. For example, when a baby is hungry she cries with hopeful anticipation in order to get her caregiver's attention with the hope the caregiver will meet that need sensitively (in an ideal situation). It has been said that attachment behaviors serve as a regulatory function and help us to regulate our distress by returning to our secure base and safe haven. Meaning, when there is a threat (for example a child skins his knee or runs into an unfriendly stranger), he seeks proximity to his mom or caregiver for comfort and support during distress. Once the child feels comforted, or as Marvin would say (Marvin & Seagroves, 2017); quoting the comic called, "Rose is Rose" by Don Wilmer and Pat Brady (Wilmer & Brady, 2002, last frame 30) the "fully charged indicator wiggle" is on, then the child is ready to launch out into the environment (out from the safety of the secure base knowing they can return there).

However, in some cases there are problems with this attachment behavioral system because the caregiving secure base and safe haven is not available, or is not safe and secure (is perhaps neglecting, abusive, etc.). Then, attachment problems arise, and an insecure or disorganized attachment style may emerge. There is room for an earned secure style to develop or the possibility of moving back to a secure pathway (Marvin, 2010; Siegel, 2011, personal communication; Steel & Steel, 2008) perhaps through other loving relationships. Attachment to God may offer one pathway, since he is available in representational and symbolic terms (as well as through the church body in concrete terms) as an attachment figure that provides both a reliable secure base and haven of safety. As Bowlby said years ago, "loss is inherently disorganizing." Every attachment relationship will eventually end in loss (perhaps either party dies, there is a divorce, or separation), but from a Judeo-Christian worldview eternity with God is conceptualized as something that does not end. It has been said that the longing for that eternal secure base and safe haven, or permanent attachment figure, is actually a yearning for the Divine Attachment Figure (DAF: Counted, 2016). It has been called by some songwriters a "God-shaped hole." A song by Plumb has lyrics that echo this thought: "there is a God shaped hole in all of us and the restless soul is searching" (Jefferson, 2017, personal communication). Based on the attachment literature and a Judeo-Christian worldview, we would postulate that the attachment wounds and attachment disappointments in life can be addressed in part by a two pronged approach that includes a relational component emphasizing relationship with God (the ultimate attachment figure) and relationship with an empathic other (perhaps a counselor, psychologist, pastor, etc.) and through therapeutic interventions that facilitating one's experience of coming to terms with the reality of his or her story (Nebrosky, 2006).

The attachment classifications can be helpful to give insight to areas to focus on in therapy, and the measure of coherence on the AAI may be something we look at to measure the progress in coherence of the story. Let's look at some of the dynamics we see in the different classifications.

BIDS FOR CONNECTION

Some authors have written about how in successful relationships partners are responsive to one another's bids for connection (Gottman, 2001; Clinton & Sibcy, 2009); however, sometimes a child may make a bid to connect with his or her parents and find that this does not accomplish the child's desired outcome. The parent does not respond to their distress in a way that comforts or helps them to regulate. This can occur because the parent is sick, depressed, overworked, or a number of other challenges that make it difficult for the parent to be available and responsive to the child. In early research on child development and object relations, influences on child development were categorized and authors such as Winnicott and Fairburn discuss the concept of whether the object is "bad" or "good enough." The objects deemed "bad" could be conceptualized by Winnicott as "not good enough" to internalize the figure. The object that has been described as bad has been indicated to stem back to the primary caregiver and to interfere with development rather than to facilitate development (creates a "rupture" that needs to be repaired). It could be described in any of the following ways "inadequate, unavailable,... abusive, and abandoning" (Kavaler-Adler, 2014) and the psychological impact of the parent is too aversive for the child to create an internal image or representation of the parent that can be integrated into the child's internal world. However, the good enough parent, though not perfect, is characterized by being responsive and sensitive to the child, though not perfect.

In chapter one of Howard Steele and Miriam Steele's book entitled, "Ten Clinical Uses of the Adult Attachment Interview", they describe one pattern of responses on the AAI, known as the Dismissing type (or D's for short in the AAI coding system). They share the idea that the dismissing speaker has firm boundaries in place that keep their attachment history that involves rejection or neglect out of the AAI discussion. There is a clear turning away from the discussion of attachment. This makes it difficult to remember whether this group can remember but chooses not to remember, or cannot remember at all about these difficult attachment experiences. When there is a turning away or a pushing away the child has the challenge then to adapt and maintain closeness to a rejecting caregiver. For example, one of our clients, Shakespeare, came to counseling with his brother and his mother after his father passed away. Shakespeare and his brother Carlos were adults. Their mother Ruby shared how she missed their father so much and how challenging the loss was. She shared a story about how when Shakespeare was a baby she would often leave Shakespeare crying in his playpen as she went out in the backyard to talk with Jake, their father. Shakespeare did not remember this experience, and when asked about his childhood, did not recall having any experiences of rejection, though he demonstrates a prototypical dismissing (Ds is short for dismissing) attachment style.

Further research on the attachment strange situation has revealed that children that display an avoidant attachment strategy are not unaffected by their attachment relationships. Physiological measures of arousal such as heart rate and cortisol has revealed that children with an avoidant attachment style demonstrate internal stress on par or above that of secure children; however, they have learned to mask that behavior and are not demonstrating the outward signs of distress as early as 12 months of age (Spangler & Grossman, 1993). Based on the research literature, it seems that the child's adaptive challenge is to maintain proximity with a rejecting caregiver. Despite the rejection from the caregiver or the insensitivity to the infant's crying, the caregiver is the source of care and provision for the infant and crying and protesting the rejection may result in further alienation. Let's consider an empathy building exercise (when it is difficult to have empathy for an dismissing (Ds) adult that may perhaps perpetuate the rejection cycle) for a Ds adult it may be helpful to picture them (in your mind's eye) as an infant crying, requesting care from a parent that is perhaps feeling overwhelmed or perhaps misperceiving the cries as antagonistic rather than as requests for care. Imagine, the baby cries for hours on end sometimes, and eventually learns (perhaps subconsciously) to mask the distress and the crying and learns that they are likely to be ignored; instead, the baby learns to turn his attention outward to toys or to other objects and away from attachment figures and the distress associated with the attachment system. We will talk more about empathy later in the text, but it is important to remember that often attachment dynamics underlie behavioral tendencies that were learned early on by a vulnerable infant, perhaps subconsciously, to deal with painful distress.

In counseling supervision we sometimes do empathy building exercises with our supervisees such as the one above, thus it may be helpful to build empathy for the rejecting or dismissing adult by picturing the baby, the infant crying alone in his crib for long stretches of time and the overwhelming feeling of distress at not being able to connect with his caregiver and to picture him finally turning away perhaps toward a teddy bear, an object, or something else for comfort. We recently travelled to Zhytomyr, Ukraine to work with and facilitate training on trauma informed treatment for a ministry called Last Bell, which provides critically important services for orphans who have never been adopted and are subsequently released from the orphanages. Some of the orphan counselors/caregivers told us that many of them have had (or have) teddy bears or objects of comfort that are very important to them.

Children are resilient and may adopt (even subconsciously) various coping strategies to deal with the pain that overwhelms them. Perhaps that it is the case with a child with avoidant attachment, who learned to give up what was natural, connecting with the other, and with great sorrow and to turn away to objects because the pain of chronic rejection had to be stifled, his heart filled with grief he turned away to objects, perhaps. Of course it is hard to know exactly what is going on in the young child beyond distress and the drive to try whatever few means he or she has to gain care from the caregiver. However, some of the studies on the details of the dynamics from the strange situation such as the study by Spangler and Grossman (1993) give us some valuable insights.

Recall that the dismissing style is an organized style, meaning an organized strategy for dealing with attachment, a turning away. So, although it is not as optimal as the secure autonomous attachment style, it is associated with more positive outcomes than the disorganized or unresolved attachment style because it is considered organized.

Another outcome of the five possible outcomes is the preoccupied, also sometimes called the ambivalent style of relating. The preoccupied style involves escalating levels of distress in order to get responsiveness from the caregiver. In the adult attachment interview this particular attachment style is usually associated with a longer transcript (in other words longer answers to the 18 interview questions which may not, still despite their length, sufficiently answer the question). The transcript and recounting of childhood experience itself may escalate, lead to exagerative or redundant speech and the speaker may get caught up in, or tangled up, in the story. It may be difficult to understand how a caregiver can be inconsistent—at times very present, loving, and available and at other times not available, role reversing, (expecting the child to care for the parent), or otherwise revealing a sense of being preoccupied or tangled up with their own experiences. In the *Handbook of Attachment,* a description that captures in part the motivation of those with an insecure anxious-ambivalent flavored style of attachment (Cassidy & Shaver, 2016, p. 40) says, "By persistently searching for an attachment figure and doing everything possible to prevent separation, the anxious-ambivalent individual increases the chance that he or she will be able to retain the attachment figure's attention and care. Thus the individual's mind is organized in a way that keeps him or her 'chronically searching' for cues regarding the attachment figures' availability and presence." I have heard manifestations of this chronic searching in attachment interviews and discussions with clients searching for an answer sometimes in the form of oscillations in a belief that a parent is loving and unloving. A preoccupied college-age female shared, "I don't understand how she could sometimes be so loving and then at other times be so neglecting. So, did she love me because she was affectionate, or did she not love me because she would abandon me for long stretches of time? I have so many questions. I wish I could just keep her in a room and not let her go until she heard everything I needed to say!"

The third organized style is the secure autonomous attachment style. With this particular style, the child exhibits protests behavior. You can see examples of this in various videos available on YouTube (search "Strange Situation" for more information). The child does not mask their distress as we see with the avoidant tendency; instead, the child actively resists the parent's departure through protest behavior. The child with a secure autonomous attachment style is more likely to be quickly soothed after reuniting with parent than children of other attachment styles. There seems to be a trust and anticipation that the others will be present and responsive.

As an adult with a secure autonomous attachment style, in the Adult Attachment Interview, the speaker is able to provide adjectives to describe their childhood experiences with caregivers and also are able to provide evidence or memories to support those particular memories. If a speaker is secure, we often hear stories that reflect a history of many experiences with a sensitive caregiver (Spangler & Grossman, 1993). Their stories are often fresh and lively and you can easily imagine them in your mind's eye. They make sense and speak in a collaborative way. In our clinical counseling work, we often use the coherence scale to measure progress (Sibcy & Knight, in progress) and are presently looking at the correlation between AAI coherence and depressive symptoms and the impact of specific interventions and treatment on both constructs. In Steele and Steele's (2008) text "Clinical Applications of the Adult Attachment Interview", there are reports of movement towards coherence. For example, the text states (2008, eBook location 150), "Chapter 10, by Massimo Ammaniti, Nino Dazzi, and Sergio Muscetta, includes three vivid case studies where repeat administrations of the AAI revealed measurable progress achieved in therapy." They specifically note that researchers have found that unresolved or disorganized cases tend to move towards an organized classification. This is very encouraging to consider the redemptive hope that we have that healing can happen and that people can move along a trajectory from an insecure or disorganized attachment style to a secure attachment style and that AAI classification can change as a function of therapy. Especially promising results are also found with Transference Focused Therapy (TFT). When individuals were diagnosed with Borderline Personality Disorder (BPD) and participated in TFT, the number with secure AAI "coherence and reflective functioning is likely to increase and the number with secure AAIs is likely to triple through TFP" (Levy et al. 2006; Cassidy & Shaver, 2016, p. 160).

Recall sometimes people incorrectly believe that one has to have had all loving experiences and a "good" childhood in order to develop a secure style. This is not the case, and we will talk more about the earned secure attachment style later in the text which is a great illustration of this.

When we have worked with clients with secure autonomous AAI transcripts and narratives in therapy, we've found them to be compelling, clear, and sometimes humorous or touching. I'm left with a clear impression of who the speaker is and a clear idea of the kind of childhood experience they had. However, even in cases where a client shares an account of their personal attachment history that is marked with loss, neglect, and other painful experiences, hope is not lost. There have been cases where a client reports few loving experiences during childhood, and yet makes sense of their experience and still comes to be able to speak of it in a relatively objective and coherent way. The speaker seems to be able to make sense of these experiences throughout the course of therapy with the use of specific strategies that we will discuss in the latter chapters of this book. The Adult Attachment interview and other assessments help us to identify the nature of a client's state of mind with respect to attachment. It is a starting point. When an insecure style or an unresolved style emerges in our clinical work, we have seen that in many situations the client has experienced many difficult experiences or psychological insults. In the subsequent chapters, we will take a look at attachment injuries and some forms of psychopathology.

CHAPTER 3 SUMMARY

The Adult Attachment Interview (AAI) is a test that is used to measure personality, mood, and many other characteristics. We call these tests "assessments." During this typically hour-long assessment the hallmark question of the AAI is asked, "Would you share with me five adjectives to describe your childhood relationship with your mother?" Each speaker is assessed in terms of the nature of their childhood experiences, their state of mind with respect to their caregivers, and experiences related to the loss of early attachment figures (including grandparents) and abuse or traumatic experiences with respect to attachment figures. Another popular instrument used to assess dimensions of attachment is the ECR. Knowing how a person personality is characterized in these terms can be of great benefit to helping the client gain an understanding of their childhood experiences and how to deal with them.

Part II

Attachment Pathologies and Scars

Part II

CHAPTER 4

Attachment Injuries and Depression

"Time may heal all wounds, but it doesn't erase the scars."

—*Jane Yolen*

In reflecting on Granqvist, Broberg, and Hagekul (2014), (which indicated *those who have a combination of religious beliefs, referred to as religiously syncretic, may use religion to compensate for harsh childhood experiences, and that perceived relationship with God may decrease risk of distress for these participants*), let's take a closer look at these childhood experiences and how they impact attachment and the maintenance of mood disorder, specifically chronic depression. *In our clinical work, we have found that these harsh experiences are also often associated with the insecure attachment classifications on the AAI* (as discussed in the previous chapter).

The discussion of attachment injuries and failures in the attachment behavioral system is reminiscent of the language and writings of Dr. James McCullough, his students, and colleagues, except they use different terminology. Let's visit some of McCullough's work and then pick back up with a Granqvist's article and integrate the two.

Dr. McCullough is a Full Professor of Clinical Psychology at Virginia Commonwealth University in Richmond, Virginia. Dr. McCullough specializes in treating and training his students and colleagues to provide effective care for clients who struggle with persistent chronic depression. Another prominent researcher in the area of chronic depression is his former student and research assistant, Dr. Jennifer Kim Penberthy (Penberthy, In Progress). Both Penberthy and

McCullough, give insightful ideas about the etiology of depression. Penberthy indicated (Penberthy, in press, P. TBA):

> "The cause of persistent depression is likely multi-factorial, and thus is best conceptualized in a bio-psycho-social framework. The influences include genetic factors, developmental history and social influences as well as coping strategies and the influence of chronic conditions such as stress or medical illness."

Some of these factors can be targeted in treatment and some of the psychological profile of the persistently depressed person is associated with early attachment experiences. In the following pages we will take a closer look at the point of intersection of attachment and persistent depression, and as this text unfolds we will look at some research based and spiritual interventions that as a part of a customized and comprehensive bio-psycho-social-spiritual treatment plan may be associated with promising outcomes.

As I was reading his book, "Treating Chronic Depression with Disciplined Interpersonal Involvement" (McCullough, 2006), he talked about Carl Rogers (Note, Carl Rogers has been referred to as the "Father of Person-Centered Psychotherapy"). McCullough discussed how when reading Rogers' text, he sensed that he was witnessing a revolution! Interestingly, as I have talked with my colleagues Dr. Gary Sibcy and Dr. Kim Penberthy, who have been trained in McCullough's approach that boasts outcomes on par with medication, I sense that I am witnessing a revolution in the treatment of chronic depression and movement from a school based way of doing therapy (i.e. Freudian, Rogerian, Adlerian, or taking the name of a theorist and turning it into an adjective by adding "ian" to the end and letting newer therapists select one approach to characterize their treatment approach) to a research-based approach. So, what makes McCullough's approach effective, and what does this have to do with attachment?

One thing that stands out to me about McCullough's approach is that it seems to facilitate neural integration by activating emotion, and likely the limbic system, while also inviting processing of that emotion and cognition by activating the pre-frontal cortex (PFC). Another aspect is the personal involvement of the therapist and the focus on desired outcomes which also activates the pre-frontal cortex. But even more importantly, I think, is the understanding and light the approach brings to the etiology of chronic depression, and herein I believe is the connection to attachment. Let's look at the explanatory model for the development of chronic depression embedded in the Cognitive Behavioral Analysis System of Psychotherapy (CBASP) approach.

In 2011, Dr. James McCullough published an article in the "American Journal of Psychotherapy" along with several of his colleagues, Benjamin Lord, Aaron Martin, Kathryn Conley, and Elisabeth Schramm. The article is called, "The Significant Other History: An Interpersonal-Emotional History Procedure Used with Early-Onset Chronically Depressed Patients." In the article, McCullough and his colleagues discuss something they refer to as *psychological insults*. Let's explore what psychological insults are and how McCullough and colleagues conceptualize the maintenance of persistent chronic depression.

McCullough and colleagues report that persistent chronic depression is maintained by the culprit of avoidance. In other words: *those who struggle with chronic depression have gotten really good at avoidance and have been practicing it a long time, especially when it comes to the interpersonal domain.* If interpersonal avoidance is the fire that keeps persistent depression burning, then fear is the gas that lights the fire. McCullough and his colleagues, such as Dr. Jennifer Kim

Penberthy, in their previous work have found that the fear is interpersonal and that it has been generalized. One of the lessons learned early on in research methods courses is the idea that large sample sizes can be more robust and give a study more power and lead to a greater case for generalization. We very rarely make generalizations based on a case study or just a few occurrences (there are some exceptions of course). However, it seems when it comes to interpersonal experiences, especially those associated with fear or anxiety, an individual may lose some objectivity and toss the rules for generalization out the window. McCullough and his colleagues share that this avoidance can be so pervasive and powerful, that it can serve the function of leading to disengagement to the point that the person struggling with chronic depression is not perceiving what is going on around them because he or she has disengaged perceptually and is no longer open to the input or new information being transmitted from observations. Instead, he or she is operating under the old data generalized from earlier experiences associated with fear that reinforce the avoidance, perhaps stemming from early psychological insults. It is as if the person is stuck on a merry go round, except the merry go round is not so merry. They are going round and round and no matter the person or situation, they see the same themes, the same view, and the same perceptions. Their lenses are blue and everything is filtered through those blue lenses of past fear and pain and that view is so pervasive that the rays of sunshine and new blooming flowers cannot be perceived, or the blue overshadows them so that they are hardly observable. McCullough and colleagues interpret this through the lens of developmental theory, specifically Piaget's approach to development that identifies this state of mind as pre-operational. They question whether clients with chronic depression would have this capacity to be empathic and to move outside of themselves in order to consider another's experience and state of mind (for more on cultivating empathy see Hawkins, Sibcy, Warren, & Knight, In progress). This leads us to the idea mentioned earlier of "psychological insults" (McCullough, Lord, Martin, Conley, & Schramm, 2011, p. 227).

The interpersonal fear that leads to avoidance is thought to be birthed from, and to develop out of, a long history of developing in a context filled with psychological insults or traumatic experiences that a person experienced from the hands of their own caregivers or significant others in their lives (McCullough, Lord, Martin, Conley, & Schramm, 2011). McCullough looks to authors such as Cichetti and Barnett (1991) that discuss how the emotional world of the child is developed through this early interpersonal context, i.e. the attachment system and in partnership with these early attachment figures. In order to understand this let's revisit the circle of security and Marvin's work (see Chapter Two for more details on the Circle of Security). Recall that when a child feels safe (typically the top part of the circle) then the exploration system is activated and the child goes out and explores his environment. When the child feels threatened or unsafe, typically he returns to the caregiver until the "fully charged indicator wiggle returns" (Marvin, 2017, pc). However, in the situation where there is abuse, trauma, or even low grade psychological insults, the source of comfort or the safe haven is also the threat. The child is wired to go to the parent when threatened or unsafe, but the parent is seen as threatening or unsafe. Therefore, the child is faced with a dilemma. The child needs the comfort that the caregiver provides, and yet it is uncertain whether that comfort will be provided or more low grade trauma/psychological insults will be inflicted. This is a very difficult and devastating situation for the small child and often the child freezes, feels distress, and has no clear strategy because there is not a clear answer for how to deal with this dilemma. For the secure child, there is a clear pathway and a sense of safety about returning to the caregiver for comfort and getting recharged. For the child that has a dismissing attachment there is a clear strategy to turn away from the caregiver and pursue independence. For the child with the preoccupied attachment to his parent, the strategy is often to become more animated and preoccupied with the attachment. However, for the child in the dilemma where the caregiver is both the source of pain and comfort from pain, there is no clear strategy. This may explain some of the reason we see many people with an abuse background (or low grade trauma/psychological insults as an adult manifesting an unresolved attachment style with respect to their parent). There may be at one point a statement that the parent was abusive and then at another point a retraction that the parent was not abusive but loving. How can a person that hurts them so much also love them? How can a parent or the person a child expects to love them most be so unloving? These may be some of the questions that haunt one who has experienced these psychological insults and are associated with the lack of coherence manifested in their Adult Attachment Interview.

Let's return to our discussion of psychological insults, McCullough, Lord, Martin, Conley and Schramm (2011, p. 227 share):

> "An aversive developmental-attachment environment, filled with years of psychological rejection from maltreating caregivers, demeaning comments or emotional neglect, is often a characteristic feature of early-onset chronic depression. These conditions may not satisfy a more traditional definition of trauma; however, like traumatic events, they contribute to the exacerbation of the early-onset disorder (Cicchetti & Barnett, 1991; Cicchetti & Toth, 1998; Hammen, 1992). It is for this reason that we have coined the term, psychological insult as being one contributory factor in the onset of childhood/adolescent chronic depression."

In other words, the emotional cradle that holds the child being one of love, delight, and responsiveness, instead is one of rejection, harsh, demeaning comments, and emotional neglect. McCullough and colleagues indicate that this unloving cradle may not meet the criteria to be considered trauma, as it may not always be physical, but the emotional wounding may cut just as deep and leave the scars of chronic depression that are visible in the interiority of the person rather than on the surface. From an attachment perspective, looking through the lens of the Adult Attachment Interview, we may call these experiences unloving and rejecting. Rejection tends to be associated with an avoidant attachment style, where one tends to "turn away" from attachment figures. This makes sense in light of the interpersonal avoidance that is said to characterize chronic depression. In terms of an unresolved or disorganized attachment style, the parent that a child wants to go to for comfort is also the source of pain or distress so the child freezes and his or her narrative of experience is disorganized as there is no clear pathway to deal with the pain of these psychological insults, the rejection, demeaning comments, and other hurtful behaviors.

Could this interpersonal avoidance that manifests in the adulthood of a client struggling with chronic depression be analogous to the freezing that happens when a child is in a threatening situation with an attachment figure? Perhaps the freezing response became so pervasive that it is also characterizing adulthood.

Note that when McCullough and colleagues discuss psychological insults, they define them as the following (McCullough, Lord, Martin, Conley, & Schramm, 2011, p. 227):

> "a continuous series of experiences, encountered by the developing child or adolescent, that are associated with interpersonal punishment/rejection and are of a 'low grade' nature; in contrast, trauma signifies one or more life threatening or

'high grade' dangers the individual experiences (e.g., sexual and/or physical abuse, actual parental abandonment, emotional or physical neglect: McCullough, 2008a; Nemeroff, Heim, Thase, Klein, Rush, Schatzberg, et al., 2003; Wiersma, Hovens, van Oppen, Giltay, van Schaik, Beekman, et al., 2009)."

In light of thinking of these psychological insults as continuous, it make sense that they would be generalized. So, although they may have been at the hands of one caregiver, they may have been many in number. These painful experiences are defined as "low grade", thus repeated rejection, unloving behavior, and demeaning remarks even though not physically threatening based on this explanatory model may have the power to trap the person in an "orbit of interpersonal sameness" and perceptually disengage them from real time experiences. However, the fear that fuels the fire of avoidance may be the result of these insults or trauma which is defined as high grade or more life threatening and can come in the form of perhaps physical abuse or emotional or physical neglect.

The felt safety, the significant other history, and the other components of CBASP keep this etiology in mind, and one can see how a sense of felt safety may be very important for one who experienced a developmental atmosphere characterized by continuous psychological insults and/or trauma. Once a client feels safe enough, the therapist can use the various CBASP interventions to connect and help disrupt the merry go round of interpersonal sameness in order to allow the client to see things anew.

With this concept of psychological insults and trauma being forces that fuel interpersonal avoidance and a trap of interpersonal sameness, let's look at the hypotheses related to attachment to God. Remember the correlational hypothesis? It makes sense that perhaps through the lens of interpersonal sameness, if one has had harsh experiences with his early caregivers, then one may have a God image that is also harsh.

The compensation hypothesis is where redemption comes into the picture! This continuous barrage of psychological insults that fire continuously on a person's heart and mind leave wounds and scars (whether visible to the eye or only on the interiority of the person). Attachment to God, as the Lover of one's soul, the Perfect Father, the one who loves with an everlasting love, Love Himself (Note in 1 John 4:8 [NIV] it says, "Whoever does not love does not know God, because God is love." Likewise, Jeremiah 31:3 [NIV] version says, "The LORD appeared to us in the past, saying: "I have loved you with an everlasting love; I have drawn you with unfailing kindness.", offers an attachment bond that supersedes all others. It is characterized by 1 Corinthians 13's perfect description of Love, and Psalms 91's perfect description of a secure base and safe haven that offers refuge from the barrage of confusing enemy fire dressed up as the caregiver . . . a clear conceptualization of a caregiver and father that offers everlasting love, forgiveness, and felt safety. Could this attachment relationship to God perhaps compensate for this barrage of psychological insults the continuous firing that trapped the person in a fearful bondage to a merry go round of interpersonal sameness? Research supporting the compensation hypothesis seems to indicate that this is a possibility; that the conceptualization and internalization of the Love of God the Father, Love Himself, and the felt safety that perhaps opens the door to His love and re-authors the attachment narrative, offers new lenses with which to look at the still world once the merry go round has stopped.

Does the felt safety lead to a stillness with which one can hear the "still small voice" and know that he or she is loved and cared for and safe? In exploration of the compensation hypothesis, we will look at some of the Scriptures and antidotes to the psychological insults associated with the development of insecure and disorganized styles and some pathways and strategies to foster a secure attachment to God the Father later in the text.

CHAPTER 4 SUMMARY

People who are religiously syncretic, or those who have a combination of religious behavior, may use religion to compensate for harsh childhood experiences. This perceived relationship with God may decrease the risk of distress for them. Dr. James McCullough's work in training his students and colleagues to treat people who struggle with persistent chronic depression and an article by Granqvist are used in this chapter as support evidence for this. Dr. McCullough's work facilitated neural integration, activating emotion and likely the limbic system while also inviting processing of that emotion and cognition, while also personally involves the therapist—all activating the pre-frontal cortex and boasts outcomes on par with medication. In an article published by McCullough and his colleagues, they discuss something they refer to as "psychological insults", which is the interpersonal fear that leads to avoidance. It is thought to be birthed from and to develop out of a long history of developing in a context filled with psychological insults or traumatic experiences that a person experienced from the hands of their own caregivers or significant others in their lives. In the situation where there is abuse, trauma, or even low grade psychological insults, then the source of comfort or the safe haven is also the threat; therefore, the child is faced with a dilemma, but there is not a clear answer for how to deal with this dilemma. The emotional cradle that holds the child instead of being one of love, delight, and responsiveness, instead, is one of rejection, harsh and demeaning comments, and emotional neglect.

The conceptualization and internalization of the Love of God the Father, Love Himself, and the felt safety that perhaps opens the door to His love and re-authors the attachment narrative, offers new lenses with which to look at the world. It is an antidote to the psychological insults associated with the development of insecure and disorganized styles and some pathways and strategies to foster a secure attachment to God the Father.

CHAPTER 5

Attachment to God and Coping

"Attachment failures lead to unprocessed feelings of unregulated grief, which, without the empathic other, create unbearable states of aloneness that can only be regulated with defenses."

—*Nebrosky (2006)*

In John 8:41–44, Jesus had the following conversation with the Pharisees:

"'You are doing the works your father did.' They said to him, 'We were not born of sexual immorality. We have one Father—even God.' Jesus said to them, 'If God were your Father, you would love me, for I came from God and I am here. I came not of my own accord, but he sent me. Why do you not understand what I say? It is because you cannot bear to hear my word. You are of your father the devil, and your will is to do your father's desires.'"

The Father's love letter version paraphrases this Scripture and puts it like this, "I have been misrepresented by those who do not know me." For some, it is a challenge to conceptualize the idea of God as a Heavenly Father, or to relate to God as an attachment figure due to misrepresentations of Him (or what a loving parent should be) in their experiences.

This is another theme from the research on attachment. Victor Counted a professor who studies the Psychology of Religion and has researched attachment found in his 2016 article, that people used their relationship with God as coping mechanisms to deal with cognitive dissonance and emotional tension (Counted, 2016, p. 333). Recently I spoke with a colleague, John Vadnal, who teaches in the School of Engineering and Computational Sciences at Liberty University, and he shared with me that he became a Christian when he was 36 years old. He shared that previously he believed that Christianity was used by people as a crutch to deal with their problems. He had heard many testimonies of people reporting a conversion experience when they hit bottom. He noted that this just confirmed his suspicion that Christianity was a crutch (and it was not until he thought about having to stand before God and giving an account for why he did not believe that he could not and the Lord revealed himself to John at the peak of his career, and John confessed he ate his own words). However, I found John's words interesting that during the time when he did not believe, he viewed the narrative of Christianity as something people leaned on in times of need. The literature reveals that people do rely on their relationship with God to cope with distress; however in some situations, they also use religious language to reinforce their own life themes related to their attachment experiences such as "Fear, abandonment, and emotional conflict" (Dykstra, 1986, p. 170).

This seems to be part of the challenge of telling ourselves the truth. One of the things that I was very much struck regarding the Adult Attachment Interview is how honest a secure autonomous narrative is. I would venture to say, perhaps, if one has had loving experiences that are congruent then it is easier to tell an honest and coherent narrative. But, oftentimes we make up lies to deal with the pain of a broken narrative. After all, would the crudeness of reality be too much to bear without sugar coating things? How difficult is it for one to say that the parent that was sometimes very loving, permitted another parent to be physically or emotionally abusive and looked the other way? Or more challenging yet, how difficult is it for one to say the parent that sometimes was loving to them, was also sometimes physically abusive to them and they still have scars to show it (perhaps both emotionally and physically). Remember, although many people may believe it is a loving childhood and positive experiences that result in a secure autonomous attachment style, this is a falsehood. Rather, it is a coherent narrative, being able to tell your story in an honest coherent way. Calling abuse, just that, abuse, without taking it back. In the Adult Attachment Interview, if a person recounts a memory where their parent abused them and describes this event, and the event is abuse, meaning it meets the criteria set forth in the AAI criteria that coders use to indicate it was indeed abuse (for example, perhaps his stepmother picked him up by the skin on his neck and threw him against the wall and the next day his neck was black and blue with a bruise. The fact that the incident left marks would be rated as abuse by clinicians who are also trained AAI coders), but then at a later time denies that he ever experienced abuse growing up, then this narrative is deemed incoherent because they indicated abuse occurred but then denied the existence of abuse. It is very difficult to say that the ones who should have been loving towards you were instead abusive. After all, to acknowledge this acknowledges the crudeness of reality.

How crude is it to be a vulnerable child without the capacity to protect oneself and to have the one you go to for protection also be the one who administers abuse? This sends a very confusing message about the world. In family systems literature, this is known as double bind communication. Double bind communication is communication where an inconsistent message is present. Some have described this as "you're darned if you do and darned if you don't" (with perhaps more colorful language than is appropriate for this text). The classic example of double bind communication is someone who invites you to come close, but then pushes you away at the same time.

Abusive experiences misrepresent God, our Heavenly Father. He is described as: the Father of all comfort (see 2 Corinthians 1:3-5, "Praise be to the God and Father of our Lord Jesus Christ, the Father of compassion and the God of all comfort, 4 who comforts us in all our troubles, so that we can comfort those in any trouble with the comfort we ourselves receive from God. 5 For just as we share abundantly in the sufferings of Christ, so also our comfort abounds through Christ.), our greatest encourager, one who loves us with an everlasting love, one who rejoices over us with singing, one who loves us so lavishly to call us his sons and daughters, one who gave himself up for us so that we could be forgiven and dwell with Him for eternity, and one who has an individual plan for each one of us that is a plan for good (Jeremiah 29:11). He is a Father who longs to do exceedingly and abundantly above all we could ask or imagine, for his thoughts towards us are countless as the sand on the seashore (Psalm 139:17). Imagine that. Have you ever taken a moment to look at the sea shore and all of those grains of sand? That is how much our Heavenly Father thinks of each one of us. Any thoughtless, careless word or action demonstrated towards one of his children is a misrepresentation of Him. Likewise, any harsh forcefulness is a misrepresentation because God is a gentleman—he does not force Himself on anyone. He stands at the door and knocks. If anyone opens the door, He will come in and sup (dine) with him.

He is right there waiting for us to, in attachment language, seek proximity to us. He wants to seek closeness to us. Our Heavenly Father longs for us to open up the door of our hearts to Him and invite Him to come in and sup with us. In this moment, as these words of your Heavenly Father's love have washed over your spirit, if your Heavenly Father has been misrepresented by fallen people, He longs for you to know His true heart and how that grieved him such. Those that hurt you will have to give an account, and woe to those who would hurt one of his little children, here is the word of caution to them (Matthew 18:6, NIV):

> "If anyone causes one of these little ones—those who believe in me—to stumble, it would be better for them to have a large millstone hung around their neck and to be drowned in the depths of the sea."

Acknowledging, quietly in your heart (you do not have to necessarily speak this out loud if you worry about the ramifications of the disclosure, though I do recommend talking to a empathic other such as a clinical mental health counselor, for referral to a professional please consult the AACC website for a list of Christian providers). He longs to be your refuge, your secure base, your strong tower that you can run to and be safe. If you do not know Him as Lord and Savior than I would invite you, dear one, to pray this simple prayer with me:

> "Heavenly Father, I believe that the Lord Jesus Christ died on the cross for my sins and paid the price for me to spend eternity in heaven with you. Come into my heart and save me. I accept you as my Lord and Savior. In Jesus' name, Amen."

If you prayed this simple prayer then I believe you were born again into the family of God. God is your Father and you have brothers and sisters in Christ. Remember they are fallen and even the best of us can in fall into sin and misrepresent Him, but I pray the crudeness of that reality leads us to discover the God shaped hole that points us always back to our Savior, who is the same yesterday, today, and forever and never disappoints [Ecclesiastes 3:11, . . . He has put eternity in the hearts of man . . .].

Recently I had the opportunity to reconnect with one of my spiritual fathers and mentors, Dr. George Jefferson. I worked as his assistant for many years and had not seen him in about seven years. He noted that he and his wife Shirley had been praying for me and the Lord gave them a Scripture to give to me. It was a Scripture I am very familiar with, but the next verse is not quoted quite as often. Let's take a look at it. It comes from the book of Jeremiah 29 and is written as a letter to the exiles, "'this is what the Lord says, 'When seventy years are completed for Babylon, I will come to you and fulfill my good promise to bring you back to this place. For I know the plans I have for you' declares the Lord, 'plans to prosper you and not to harm you, plans to give you hope and a future. Then you will call on me and come and pray to me, and I will listen to you. You will seek me and find me when you seek me with all your heart. I will be found by you,' declares the Lord, 'and will bring you back from captivity. I will gather you from all the nations and places where I have banished you' declares the Lord, 'and will bring you back to the place from which I carried you into exile (Jeremiah 29:10-14).'" This is an invitation from the Lord to seek him and find him when we search for him with all of our hearts. We are called to seek proximity to our Heavenly Father. In a latter chapter, we will discuss proximity seeking, but note one strategy for seeking closeness to God is prayer. Note the Psalmist David has sought proximity to God and often poured out his heart. He acknowledged how he was persecuted, he commanded his soul to praise God, and he was very honest about his feelings. Yet, David is known as a man after God's own heart. He must rest in the assurance, that God wants us to share our narratives with Him. After all, He already knows our narratives. He is the author of redemption. He can ensure that the second half is better than the first.

Those who may have experienced abuse and heartache and encountered much representation may find hope in these truths:

1. The promise of Isaiah 61:7 (NIV) inspires hope for restoration and everlasting joy. Consider the words of this passage:

   "Instead of your shame you will receive a double portion, and instead of disgrace you will rejoice in your inheritance. And so you will inherit a double portion in your land, and everlasting joy will be yours."

2. The best is yet to come as (1 Corinthians 2: 9-10) talks about the idea that the poet, Bobby Burns eloquently writes about. Consider the words of this scripture:

   "However, as it is written: 'What no eye has seen, what no ear has heard and what no human mind has conceived'[b]—the things God has prepared for those who love him—these are the things God has revealed to us by his Spirit."

3. Difficulties that we overcome will work something positive in the life of the believer. Consider the passage that reminds us of end working of suffering in the believer's life is character and hope (Romans 5: 1–5, NIV):

   "Therefore, since we have been justified through faith, we[a] have peace with God through our Lord Jesus Christ, 2 through whom we have gained access by faith into this grace in which we now stand. And we[b] boast in the hope of the glory of God. 3 *Not only so, but we[c] also glory in our sufferings, because we know that suffering produces perseverance; 4 perseverance, character; and character, hope.* 5 And hope does not put us to shame, because God's love has been poured out into our hearts through the Holy Spirit, who has been given to us.

Part of renewing our minds is meditating on the comfort and truth of God's word, which also reminds us that He is our Comforter. The scripture also discusses promises of overcoming. When thinking of the difficulties experienced or the challenges of having to overcome a harsh God image and do the work of replacing it with an image of a compassionate and loving God, it is helpful to remember that He rewards his children. Consider the words of James:

"He who overcomes receives the crown of life" (James 1: 12, NIV).

Perhaps, we have the capacity to extend "The Blessing" that John Trent and Gary Smalley talk about, despite not having received it. *It has been said that: grace says you can give what you have not gotten.*

Here are some truths the Lord has put on our hearts to share with you (we have written them in the format of a poem), may we all come into a greater knowledge of how great, deep and wide the love of God is for us as we mediate on Him and His loving. This is especially for those whose former days were fraught with attachment injuries and psychological insults, the same truths hold true for sons of God, but this was particularly written for daughters who may have encountered sexual abuse or other psychological insults.

Oh dear Daughter of the King, here are some words from your Father to bring you hope and a rope out of the deep pit of despair:

Remember, the sweet is never as sweet without the bitter, my dear you have had your fill of much bitterness, so how sweet must your latter days be! Sweeter than sweet can be!

The Giver of life and light is at your side, from Him you will never have to hide.

Your heart was broken and shattered, but he mended it into something more beautiful than before. For He is the master restorer.

He brought beauty from the ashes of your life, the oil of joy from your morning and has given you the spirit of adoption. As your heart cries, *Abba Father,* he responds, *"You are my beloved Daughter."*

CHAPTER 5 SUMMARY

For some, it is a challenge to conceptualize the idea of God as a Heavenly Father or to relate to God as an attachment figure due to misrepresentations of Him (or what a loving parent should be) in their experiences. Counted (2016) found that people used their relationship with God as a coping mechanism to deal with cognitive dissonance and emotional tension. Some view the narrative of Christianity as something people leaned on in times of need.

However, those that experience double bind communication, that is, communication where an inconsistent message from a caregiver is present, can, because of this, have notions about God that are actually misrepresentations of God. In fact, He is right there waiting for us to, in attachment language, seek proximity to us.

CHAPTER 6
God Attachment

"How precious to me are your thoughts, God! How vast is the sum of them!
Were I to count them, they would outnumber the grains of sand—
when I awake, I am still with you."

—Psalm 139:17–18

Returning to the research literature on attachment to God, a theme that stood out was the idea that if a participant indicated a perceived relationship with God, this may be associated with a decrease in distress (Counted, 2016). This aforementioned speculative conclusion from the peer-reviewed research is very encouraging because it provides hope to speculate or hypothesize that people can embrace a relationship with God as a pathway to find healing from the distress of attachment injuries or insensitive/unavailable attachment figures. Research reveals that when people relate to God as "paraclete" (Counted, 2016, p. 336) which is frequently substituted for a Hebrew word "naham". The Hebrew word "naham" (Counted, 2016, p. 336) is said to mean sympathy and this focus on one of God's attributes, his kindness and compassion (see Psalm, 135:13–14) has been associated as a way of relating to God that helps one to find meaning and healing in experiences.

Let's consider what some scientist practitioners have found in the way of physical evidence that this finding (that relationship with God can be a pathway to healing) is true. Neuroscientists and psychiatrists using Single-Photon Emission Computed Tomography (referred to as SPECT for short) imaging have found manifestations of this in the brain imaging work they have seen! You may be wondering what SPECT imaging is. A full psychiatric evaluation that includes a SPECT is typically not reimbursed by insurance. SPECT is similar to an FMRI in that it provides an image of what is going on inside of the brain, but the patient does not have to go into as narrow of a machine, so people struggling with symptoms of claustrophobia may be more comfortable with this. The Amen Clinics boast over 100,000 SPECTs from over 111 countries (September, 2017 from http://www.amenclinics.com/faq/) and they report that the SPECT illustrates areas of the brain that work well, areas of the brain that do not work well, and areas of the brain that work too hard. The Amen clinics report that they opt to use SPECT rather than fMRIs because they are less costly. All Amen physicians have been trained personally by Dr. Daniel Amen who has been conducting this research for over 26 years and has written or co-authored with colleagues in more than 70 peer-reviewed research studies!

One of my colleagues that works at Amen clinics shared that if a client with PTSD would participate in meditation, then it would calm down areas of the brain associated with the PTSD (D. Kalyanapu, personal communication, June 2, 2015). I asked her if this would be the same if this could be adapted for our Christian clients, perhaps, if a Christian wanted to do this and wanted to participate in prayer. She smiled and shared, "It depends on what type of prayer. If it is the type where you are talking to God, then no." I asked, "What about contemplative prayer?"

She said, "What is that?"

I said, "It involves being still and quiet, and meditating on a phrase, word or scripture (like Jesus, peace, love, etc.) and quieting the mind and contemplating that and listening."

She said, "That would be helpful in changing the brain if you are quiet and meditating on the phrase." Amen clinics have the largest collection of SPECT's (recall SPECTs are brain images) of any medical facility and Amen doctors know what to look for and what has led to changes in the brain based on their research and imaging work. Therefore, this was exciting to hear. We will talk more about contemplative prayer later.

In the "Journal of Religion and Health", an article was published that was entitled, "Spirituality and Religiosity and its Role in Health and Diseases" in August of 2017 by Shri Mishra and colleagues. In this article the authors state that religiosity (when conceptualized as multidimensional in nature) is associated with "protection against diseases and overall better quality of life" (Mishra, Togneri, Tripathi, & Trikamji, 2017, p. 1282). Mishra and colleagues indicate that many studies have confirmed that religiosity plays a role in health outcomes (Mishra, Tongenri, Tripathi, & Trikamji, 2017, p. 1282; Greely and Hout, 2006; Haslan et al. 2009; Ironson, et al, 2002, Hummer et al., 1999). There is even a new and emerging field that specifically explores the correlation between religious practices and changes in the brain. It is called Neuroethology (Newberg, 2014). Newberg utilized SPECT imaging (the same neural imaging procedure that the Amen clinics use), to evaluate the impact of centering prayer on three nuns and found less blood flow in what was referred to as the "orientation area" (Mishra, Togneri, Tripathi, & Trikamji, 2017, p. 1282; Newberg, 2011). This is the area located in the temporal lobe that is involved in a human's sense of self and his or her surroundings. In addition, they report physical health benefits between spirituality and a number of health benefits such as reduced blood pressure (Hixson et al., 1998), decreases in occurrences of psychiatric disorders, and substance abuse problems in more religious participants.

Even the link between spirituality and mental and physical health has been established, more work needs to be done to specify more about the mechanisms of change and researchers recommend double blind studies.

Kirkpatrick (2005) has been a key player in the literature on spirituality, specifically God attachment. His work supports the idea of God (the Christian God) as an attachment figure. In the next chapter we will discuss more about some of the themes that have emerged throughout the God attachment literature.

CHAPTER 6 SUMMARY

This chapter deals with the idea that if a person has a perceived relationship with God and spiritual disciplines such as meditation and prayer, this may be associated with a healing pathway that leads to a decrease in distress. This is tangibly shown in experiment using SPECT used by doctors such as Dr. Daniel Amen of the Amen clinics. Although, the link between spirituality and mental and physical health has been established, more work needs to be done to specify more about the mechanisms of change. Researchers recommend double blind studies for this.

CHAPTER 7

The Importance of Story Telling: Training the Narrator and Research Based Treatments for Attachment Injuries

"Storytelling is about patience, about making sense of the moments of pathos and beauty that you find, and about carrying these moments back into your own life."

— *Michael Paterniti*

When I was younger I recall listening to a radio show each day by the late Paul Harvey where he would tell what he called *"the rest of the story."* Some parts of Harvey's stories were revealed at the end of the broadcast and listeners developed a better understanding of the content. When it comes to personal stories, as counselors help clients facilitate their narrative or enhance what is known as their "autobiographical competence", they are helping their client in a sense tell, what Paul Harvey would have called, "the rest of the story."

As we discussed in "Chapter 3: Measuring your Attachment Style: The Gold Standard" we discussed the AAI and that there are some distinguishing features of someone with a secure narrative. The primary indicator of a person with a narrative that is rated secure autonomous on the AAI is called coherence. One of the most distinguishing features of their story about their early childhood experiences is that the story makes sense, that the way it is relayed is congruent and coherent, and it is not fraught with contradictions. Evidence must be provided to support claims, that are consistent, and the reader or listener is not confused about the content of the story. Some may be surprised that it is not about whether their experiences are good or bad per say, but it is about their capacity to describe those experiences accurately. In Howard Steel and Miriam Steel's text, "Clinical Applications of the AAI", they discuss the importance of secure attachment in predicting a host of positive outcomes in life and the idea that *if an individual was not blessed enough to have had a sensitive attachment system during childhood, then:*

> *"Various compensatory pathways can be charted so that mental health comes to be achieved by way of the human capacity to seek out care, accept it, and in turn provide care in ways that were not previously familiar to the individual.* These "ways" seem to involve interactions with a new relationship partner (e.g. a spouse) or a caregiving figures (e.g. a therapist) who helps one arrive at new understandings of old troubles . . ." (Steel & Steel, 2008, p. 44).

Speakers who have an earned secure attachment classification will typically have experienced adverse childhood experiences, or at least less loving experiences than their continuous secure counterparts because their loving scores must be 3 or less on the AAI, which represents experiences in childhood attachment relationships where they experienced instrumental love, but no special dedication, warmth, affection or stronger forms of love. Acknowledging a lack of love or even unloving or difficult experience where loving experiences may be expected can be very challenging to face. An article by Glenn Roisman and his colleagues (Roisman, Padron, Sroufe, & Egeland, 2002) on Earned-Secure attachment status opened with a powerful quote: *"I had a weak father, domineering mother, contemptuous teachers, sadistic sergeants, destructive male friendships, emasculating girlfriends, a wonderful wife, and three terrific children. Where did I go right?"*—Jules Feiffer, illustrator and satirist. This quote is thought to capture part of the experiences of the earned secure attachment status which represent difficult early relationships but somehow manage to develop secure tendencies. Typically, there is someone who as my friend from Switzerland mentioned, ". . . showed them what love is." Perhaps, this makes it easier to bear the crudeness of the reality that is involved in sharing a narrative regarding unloving childhood experiences.

DEVELOPING A COHERENT ACCOUNT OF OUR ATTACHMENT HISTORY

"Perhaps the most important revelation is precisely this:
that left cerebral hemisphere of humans is prone
to fabricating verbal narratives that do not necessarily accord with the truth."

—*Antonio Damasio*

Telling a story about a painful experience requires skill.

Coherence is defined as "systematic or logical connection and consistency" (Merriam-Webster, nd). One challenge regarding consistency can be the difficulty of telling a story that involves inconsistency. For example, when a long-time client I had, Darla, discussed her relationship with her father; she used the adjective "inconsistent" and when prompted to support the word she chose she shared that he was sometimes very loving and spent time helping her with homework. When probed for a specific situation Darla recounted a time that her father stood up for her when Darla was having difficulty with a teacher. She went on to explain, "The teacher kicked me out of the classroom for talking to another student when it was not me; it was the guy behind me! And I thought that was loving because my father believed me and told the teacher she was wrong. On the other hand, he could also be very unloving. After the divorce, he remarried a woman that did not seem to like me much and she was very strict and would sometimes hit me and leave bruises. Even though he saw the bruises and knew how they got there, he never said anything to her when she hit us . . . he just looked the other way. That felt very unloving and confusing. So you see, it was inconsistent, sometimes loving and sometimes unloving. Wow, I never thought about it until now—but it was very polarized, this inconsistency did not happen until after he remarried when I was seven."

Darla's narrative above is fairly coherent despite being what some may consider a difficult truth to come to terms with and discuss freely. From an attachment measurement perspective, there are several things that are important for a speaker to be able to share a coherent story of his or her early personal relationships or attachment history. Coherence of transcript is measured on a 9 point scale, and is the top predictor, as mentioned previously, of attachment security. In our clinical work to target improvements in chronic depression symptomatology and facilitate movement towards attachment security (Sibcy & Knight, in progress), we use the Adult Attachment Interview (AAI) and look closely at coherence. Our aim is to see increases in coherence of narrative. In other words, we want to see that a client is able to make progress in being able to tell their story in a consistent and congruent manner.

Therefore, attachment researchers look to Grice's maxims of communication for criteria to evaluate the coherence of one's story of their attachment history (Grice, 1975, 2008). Grice's work indicates that effective communicators should obey the cooperative principle. Honoring the cooperative principle means that when communicating the speaker and listener use Grice's maxims of collaborative communication in order to both encode and decode information. As we seek to help clients tell their stories and enhance the coherence of their autobiographical narrative, employing strategies that help them to become more collaborative speakers is important (or good story tellers of their attachment histories). The maxims include: quantity, quality, relevance, and manner.

Let's look at each of Grice's maxims of collaborative communication and how they may be attended to in order to help a client narrate their attachment story. The maxim of quantity refers to the length of the communication. *In order for a message to honor this maxim of quantity, a message should be as informative as possible but not more informative than necessary* (Koch, Forgas, and Matovic, 2013). For example, when checking in with a client about how they connected with their father growing up, I might start by asking, "Would you tell me what adjectives you would use to describe your relationship with your father, who raised you, as a child?" If the client says, "I can't think of any." This response would not be considered collaborative because they are not providing an answer given that the client grew up with his father and would be expected to be able to tell his therapist a bit about his father. Since this would not be an assessment intervention, but a therapeutic intervention, the therapist may exhibit some empathy and then offer some assistance by saying, "It can be difficult to think back to before 12 years of age."

The maxim of quality requires truthfulness and reliability (Koch, Forgas, and Matovic, 2013). When I work with graduate students on developing their research projects, I always ask them to make sure and seek to support assertions with citations, or supporting evidence that provides information that explains the findings or data to support a certain conclusion or idea. Cognitive Behavioral Therapists therapists tend to do this regularly. Consider the process of examining the veracity of a negative thought. We may draw a thought chart on a whiteboard and ask questions similar to those Byron Katie outlines in her book called, "Loving What Is," where after allowing the participant to be as honest and judgmental about a difficult thought the questions begin (Katie, 2002, p. 296). The first question is, "Is [the thought] true?" The second question is, "Can you absolutely know that [the thought] is true?" The third question is, "How do you react when you think that thought?" (Sometimes these additional questions are used here: "Can you find a reason to drop the thought?" and "Can you find a stress free reason to keep this thought? This lie?") The last question of Byron Katie's "The Work" program is, "Who would you be without this thought?" I prefer these to the other common phrasing to examine negative or problematic thoughts such as "What evidence do you have for the thought?" And "What evidence do you have against the thought?" This series of questions really helps a person to contemplate the reality of their thought, the veracity of their thought, and the evidence for or against it. This practice of examining thoughts and looking at what evidence we have for any given source of information can be very helpful. In between, of course, in a very kind and compassionate manner and with terms of endearment Katie may work others through their interpretations back to reality by gently inviting them to focus on the truth. I also really enjoy my colleague, Dr. Gary Sibcy's strategy for helping people move away from interpretations and back to the facts of a situation. He sometimes uses expressions like, "If I was a fly on the wall, what would I see?" (Sibcy, 2016, personal communication). If a client still persists with discussing how he or she felt about or interpreted a situation rather than just the events (as is required with a situation analysis) then he may further redirect the client by saying, "I'm feeling like a lost ball in high weeds over here! I am trying to figure out what happened: what is the beginning, middle, and end of the story?" The situation analysis is a strategy that is a part of CBASP (a research supported treatment for chronic depression), which we will discuss in more detail here.

The CBASP approach has several components, one is the Situation Analysis, which involves asking a client a series of questions to help them identify what their desired outcome was in a given situation, the actual outcome that their behavior achieved for them, and the difference between the two (in addition to helping them understand that they do have the capacity to influence their behavior). Let's look at a clinical example, that we'll call "The passive depressed counselor-pastor" that shows how early attachment injuries can manifest in the form of chronic depression, and then how the depressed mode can be maintained by current behaviors (or lack thereof). We like to use tools such as EAR, situation analysis, and interpersonal discrimination exercises. Below let's discuss these interventions and their application in therapy.

JOHN: THE COUNSELOR–PASTOR STRUGGLING WITH PASSIVITY AND DEPRESSION

After having a really good therapy session one week, the following week John said he was kind of "up and down." The therapist encouraged him to elaborate some. John responded, "Well, it was pretty good for the next few days. Then I had a lot of anxiety and tension about how to manage my time for the weekend. I wanted to do some yard work but I also had to prepare a sermon. And my wife asked me to take a check to the bank when she was going right by the bank on her way to work. I got everything done but I was tired and down the whole time. Then on Monday (a holiday) I wanted to spend the evening with my wife but our house guest was home the entire evening and spoiled my plans.

The next morning I woke up feeling completely depressed. It makes me wonder if therapy is really helping me. I just wonder if what we are doing is really helping me. We keep going over communication style but how is that related to my depressed mood.

Let's pause for a moment and consider what is happening. Although, some therapists may conceptualize this response (questioning the efficacy of therapy) as resistance or find that their internal response is one of defensiveness, we do not see this as helpful here. Let's conceptualize this scenario in terms of attachment and think about the client's negative comment through these lenses. Here is how we conceptualize it:

First of all, this is clearly an activation of John's internal working models. Remember that the attachment system serves to regulate emotions, and from the cradle to the grave when one is feeling anxious or in need of recharging, it is helpful to be able to get sensitive support from an attachment figure (in adulthood we turn from parents to friendships or romantic partners for attachment figures). Recall from previous chapters, we discussed how internal working models relate to relationship rules such as "Am I worthy of love?" and "Are others competent to show me love?" (Clinton & Sibcy). Perhaps, since John's wife did not pick up on his needs or was not as intuitively sensitive as he would have liked, he took this as confirmation that the answer to one or both of his relationship rules was no (i.e. no you are not worthy of love, or no, others are not able to love you).

John is on the bottom of the cycle, of what Bob Marvin would call the Circle of Security or we could also say he is low on the attachment temperature gauge (recall that John Bowlby compared the attachment behavioral system to a thermometer, so to be cold or to have a low battery, as Marvin may say, the person is in need of some charging and safety). If we interpret John's questioning of therapy as defensiveness or a personal affront and respond in a less than empathic way then we lose a powerful therapeutic opportunity. Instead let's look at using the therapeutic strategy that can be represented with an acronym EAR. Ear represents: empathy, assertiveness and respect.

In order to respond appropriately to John's concern, we need to use good communication skills and good counseling skills. Dr. David Burns in his book entitled, "Feeling Good Together" describes these skills with the acronym EAR. EAR is an acronym that stands for: empathy, assertiveness, and respect. This acronym is also helpful in training novice therapists to think about the ear (the part of the body we listen with) and how these words can represent some of the principles of helpful listening and communication.

Let's take this opportunity to examine each component and then we will return to John's case. Empathy comes first in this acronym, and we believe it is the most important feature of strong listening skills. As a matter of fact, we believe so much in this principle that it is the focus of some of our research and writing. We are in the process of co-authoring with several of our colleagues (Dr. Ron Hawkins and Dr. Steve Warren) a text on the importance of empathy and attachment-based developmental conceptualizations of the counseling skills (see Hawkins, Sibcy, Knight, & Warren, in press). Recall, that in previous discussions on attachment, it was noted that a failure in the skill of empathy is a key contributor to attachment injuries, thus it is important to use high levels of authentic empathy when facilitating the confrontation of the truth in a difficult attachment story. Burns defines empathy as, "Listening and trying to see the world through the other person's eyes" (Burns, 2008, p. 71). This action step to manifest this empathy in communication is through the reflective listening skills. It requires reflecting the content of what the other person (in this case John) is saying, and searching for a kernel of truth. Our friend, Randy Miller, who is a phenomenal research librarian sometimes compares this process to his time spent living in the midwest and seeing many cow patties. Randy shares that there is usually a visible kernel of corn in those cow patties, just like there is usually a kernel of truth in every "pile of poo" that we are handed. So, this may stink and it may require some hunting, but it is an important part of the process of communicating empathy. This requires giving up our right to be understood for a moment and seeking to understand. Therefore, even if the client's perspective is different from our own—the complaint is about therapy, etc., it is our task to find the kernel of truth, (in this case John has concern regarding the efficacy of counseling) and reflect that back in a compassionate way.

The next part of the EAR equation, after empathy, is assertiveness. Burns describes the manifestation of assertiveness as involving sharing our feelings in a polite and tactful manner so that they are easier for the other person to digest. This comes into play with the interpersonal discrimination exercise as well.

The last part of the EAR acronym after empathy and assertiveness is respect. Let's start with respect in terms of valuing and validation. For example, we may respond with, "I'm really glad you asked that . . . That's a really important question and I want you to feel like you can voice these kind of concerns in here." The respect component, as Burns describes it, involves relating to the other person with an attitude that is characterized by kindness even though we may be feeling irritated (remember, that if heart rate rises above 100 beats per minute and a person becomes flooded, they may need a break or time out in order to be able to effectively engage in respectful and empathic communication).

If we applied the addition of empathy with inquiry to John's case, we would respond with, "It sounds like what you're asking is if the things we are talking about in here, the communication stuff and looking at these relational events is related to the feelings of depression you get." (Notice, this is an application of reflecting listening skills that most counselors learn in their counselor skills training course that can be effectively increased through strategic practice (Knight, 2009)).

John responds by elaborating (which may be indicative of a sense of felt safety), "Yes, I just woke up on Tuesday feeling totally down and depressed. I didn't feel like going to work I felt like 'What's the point? Why am I so tired? I'm just not getting any better.'"

The therapist using the EAR communication method may then respond to John as follows, "Okay, so when you woke up on Tuesday feeling so down and depressed you couldn't figure out why you were feeling that way, and began to wonder about how the things we're talking about here in therapy is related to the way you're feeling. That is such an important question and I hope that by what we cover here today you'll be able to see that more clearly." Notice here the therapist is validating the question and expressing assertive feeling "I hope . . ."

The therapist then goes onto continue using EAR and the empathic listening skills, "Let me see if I can summarize what happened this weekend. You had a pretty good week until you got to

Friday when you were somewhat stressed about how to manage your time: you wanted to get some yard work done but you also needed to prepare a sermon. Then, your wife asks you to take the check to the bank. You knew that she was going to go right by the bank on her way into town and could easily drop off the check. If I understand correctly, you didn't say anything to her about this but just took the check and dropped it off even though you had a bunch of stuff you needed to get done. Is that accurate?"

John paused for a moment, "Yes," he responded.

The counselor continued reflecting what was heard with empathy and respect, "Then you got everything else done that needed to be completed over the weekend, including entertaining some out-of-town missionaries Sunday night. But on Sunday you wanted to relax with your wife and have some intimate time with her but this was foiled by the fact that your in-house guest decided to stay home that evening as well. And if I'm understanding correctly, you didn't say anything to your wife about what your plans were."

"That's right," he said, "I didn't say anything."

Here we have a sense of John's response that is passive. So, we would continue to implement a CBASP approach to therapy, called the situation analysis. Let's look at how we may do this with our client, John.

"John, if we can, I'd like for us to examine this event through our CBASP Situation Analysis lens and then talk about how this is relevant to your concern. What is your comfort level with this?"

"I feel comfortable with it," he agreed and so we completed the following situation analysis. As you will see there are seven steps to the CBASP situation analysis: (1) situation, (2) interpretation, (3) behavior description, (4) actual outcome, (5) desired outcome, (6) comparison of actual and desired outcomes, and (7) causal conclusion analysis. Each step will make more sense to you the reader as we cover them in the case below. Here are a couple of important points to keep in mind. The situation is a description of a concrete relationship interaction between the client and another person. This situation is specific, occurring at some place at some time, with a beginning, middle, and in point. It is sometimes referred to as a little slice of time. Another important point about the situation description is that you are asking the client to simply describe the facts of the situation without including his interpretations and commentary on the event. This is quite challenging for people because in normal conversation people tend to intertwine the description of facts with commentary. For nondepressed people, they are typically able to distinguish between their interpretation of an event and the event itself. However for those who are depressed and those who suffer from various forms of insecure attachment, the ability to separate fact from interpretation is impaired. So asking them to separate the two so that in in step one they only give the facts, describing the relational interaction and in step two they give their interpretations.

Also, an important part of the situation description is to identify the endpoint as being a specific behavior executed by the client. This endpoint will be used as the Actual Outcome later, in step four. An outcome in this model is some behavior that is 100% under the control of the person. This is important because we will also examine the Desired Outcome in step five, which is asking the client that if he could go back in time and change the actual outcome, what would he replace it with? Or would he keep it the same?

Let's take a look at the situation.

SITUATION: wife asked me to take check to the bank. I ask her if she's going by the bank on her way into town this morning. She said yes but that she didn't want to stop because she had so much to do today at work. I said, "okay," and drop it.

We identify the underlined sentence as the actual outcome (AO). In this situation analysis,

INTERPRETATIONS:

1. It's not like I'm not busy

2. She really doesn't care about my concerns; what I want doesn't matter.

3. Just do it to make her happy

BEHAVIORS: I asked in a normal tone if she was going by the bank. Then I said in a normal tone, "okay I'll do it." Then I dropped it and didn't say anything else.

ACTUAL OUTCOME: I ended up taking the check to the bank even though I had more than what she had to do.

I said, okay, and dropped it.

DESIRED OUTCOME: for her to drop off a check.

DID YOU GET THE DESIRED OUTCOME? No

WHY? Because people just don't take me seriously.

After he had finished completing this form, I asked him to go back over it with me so we could highlight some important aspects.

Let's go over what you have on this form and I want to draw your attention to the desired out-come. You wrote, "for her to drop off the check." Is that an outcome that you have 100% control over?

I don't think so.

I think you're right. Neither you nor I have control over what other people do. But my question is if you want your wife to drop off the check, and you look back at your behavior in the situation—where you said "okay" and dropped the topic—is there any way your wife could have known that you wanted her to drop off the check?

I guess not. But I shouldn't have to tell her. She should know that I want to get things done around the house, that we have people visiting for the weekend, and that I have to write my sermons on Friday. Plus, she was going by the bank herself. Why couldn't she just simply drop off the check?

I agree 100%. If we lived in a perfect world where people always do what they should do, I think you're right. I call this perfect world, Shouldville. In Shouldville you never have to tell people how you feel, what you want, and what you don't want. They just get it. And they always respond to the way they should. Perhaps in Shouldville your wife would have sensed your stress and would have never asked you to take the check to the bank in the first place. But, we live in Realville. In this imperfect world, we actually have to tell people how we feel and what we want or don't want. Otherwise, they just won't get it. And even when we do tell them, they may not respond the way they should.

Howard, when you don't speak up, what's the price you pay?

I don't know . . .

I don't know either, for sure. But, a really important part of our work is helping you realize that what you do and what you don't do both have consequences. They affect you and your body. Your body keeps the score. When you don't speak up your brain concludes, "What's the point? What's the use? I just give up." Then the brain proceeds to shut off the chemistry you need for energy, motivation and pleasure. Your brain thinks, "Hey, if you aren't going to do things that use this chemistry designed for energy motivation and pleasure, then I'm going to stop making it."

"Yes, but what's the point in trying to say anything to her because she just won't listen. Just like everybody in my life they just don't take me seriously."

"We don't know for sure how she will act if you tell her what you want, what you need, what you feel. But it's like a baseball player who goes to the plate. What is his desired outcome?"

"To get a hit."

"Well, his goal is to get a hit. But that can't be his desired outcome because getting a hit is not directly under his control. If he wants to get a hit, what does he absolutely have to do in order to make that happen?"

"I guess swing the bat."

"That's right. He has to take good swings at good pitches. Now just because he takes good swings at good pitches doesn't mean he will get a hit every time. The best batters only get a hit three out of every 10 at-bats. But it does give him the best opportunity for getting a hit. If he doesn't swing the bat and goes down on called strikes, he will walk away feeling defeated. Depression doesn't come from swinging the bat and missing but from not swinging at all.

So if you want your wife to know what you want, what would you have said, what would have been a good swing?"

"Honey, I'd love to help you out today but I have a lot on my plate and I'm kinda stressed out about it. Can you just drop it off on your way in to town?"

"That's fantastic. I especially like the fact that on the front end of that statement you made it clear that you would like to help her and you called her 'honey,' which says, 'I value you.'"

Howard and I continue to work through the situation, helping him see that the primary reason he did not obtain his desired outcome was because he did not engage in the kind of assertive behavior needed for his wife to even know what he needed or wanted. We also spent some time focusing on what kind of thoughts he would need to produce in order to speak up and tell her what he needed. But then we turned our attention to Howard's initial concern about whether treatment was really focusing on the things he needs. I wanted to address this in two ways: First, to help him see that by focusing on interpersonal situations and how he handles it will go a long way in helping him resolve his chronically depressed mood. The second was to focus on revising his internal working model which says nobody takes me seriously. I can't speak up and tell people what I want or question what people do without being rejected, criticized, or shamed. This model was formed in his early relationships, especially with the stepfather and has been transferred to his current relationships (wife, boss and colleagues) and in therapy.

The best way to address this internal working model is through the Interpersonal Discrimination Exercise, which is illustrated below.

"John, let me ask you a question: we discussed this some when we did the significant other history. But when you were young and you questioned your stepdad, when you asked him why you had to do what you are doing, or you objected to something, how would he respond?"

"Oh. It was bad! He had a flaming temper. He would go off."

"What kind of things would he say?"

"He'd be very belittling, making me feel like I was totally stupid and incompetent. It wasn't like he'd curse at me, but his face would get all mad and flustered. He would yell, pointed his finger at me, and spit would fly out of his mouth. He got a little crazy."

"And how would you feel in that situation when he did that?"

"Awful really. Like . . . I was a total idiot. I learned pretty early it's best to just keep my mouth shut."

"So, what kind of feeling did you get though? Were you anxious, scared, ashamed?"

"Yeah, he had a way of twisting things around so I was being selfish for even bringing up a topic that made him feel uncomfortable. Even when he didn't get all angry and flustered and red-faced, he had a way of belittling me with his condescending tone. You could just sense anger he was holding back."

"Again, how would you feel when he did this?"

"Like a complete idiot for bringing up the topic in the first place. It was like I was being a selfish."

"Oh, I see, so you felt like an idiot for challenging him or a selfish pig for wanting something different than what he wanted?"

"Right. Exactly."

"Now I'm wondering about today, when you asked about what we were doing in here and if it was the right thing."

"Oh, I wasn't challenging your approach, Dr. Sibcy."

"I'm not saying you were, but you were concerned and wondering if we were doing the right stuff for you and here. Which I think is good. But I'm wondering, how did I respond to that?"

"Well . . . You said it was good that I asked about it and then we talked about the weekend using that form. You helped me see that not speaking led to my depressed mood."

"How was what I did different than your dad, when you challenged him or questioned him?"

"You didn't get all mad and flustered."

"Okay, good, I didn't feel that way either. I was delighted by the fact that you had the courage to ask me about what we were doing and if it was the right thing. To me that suggested you were taking an active part in your treatment. John, can I belittle you and make you feel like an idiot like you are being selfish?"

"Now, not at all."

"What do you think this says about our relationship?"

"That I can ask questions and bring up concerns without feeling like you're going to go off at me."

"And what do you think this says about other relationships . . . Down the road?"

"I don't know . . ."

"Well, is it possible that there might be others, down the road, who might also be open to hearing about your concerns or wants and needs without belittling you were making you feel selfish?"

"I suppose so."

"I think all of those apply. So you came to learn from your stepdad that to question him or to speak up led to feeling really badly?"

"Yeah, I'd say that's right."

Notice, how in the above case with John the therapist was encouraging him to answer questions in a collaborative way, and focus on the requirements of the question and to make sense of experience in a systematic way. This is consistent with Grice's maxims of communication that are required for coherent attachment stories, and thus are required for a person to make sense and confront the truth of their story.

Grice's last maxim of collaborative communication is especially relevant in the situation analysis. In addition for the need for a story to be the correct length (sufficient to provide needed information, but not also including too much extra information) and to have evidence to support it, another one of Grice's maxims of communication is relevance, that is providing only information that is relevant to the discussion at hand. *When discussing one's attachment **history** then, it is important to keep the conversation focused on the **past***. (However, please note that this just means talking about the appropriate time period, and that a secure speaker still has a narrative that is characterized by a mindfulness associated with the present moment). If using Byron Katie's questions to examine a problematic thought, it is important to stay with the questions. In therapy many times we only have 50 minutes to an hour, so there is not much time for extraneous information or a client may be on a circuitous route to making progress in treatment. Recall

Grice's maxims require some degree of mindfulness that the other person is there rather than being so overwhelmed by the process of uncovering an experience as to forget about the other person and the time frame. The strategies discussed so far may be tools to use to help a client develop mindful and collaborative communication skills that can set the stage for the unfolding of a coherent narrative.

The last maxim of collaborative communication is manner (Grice, 1975). *Honoring the maxim of manner in collaborative communication involves a speaker being able to focus on the relevant information and be both brief and orderly.* This involves striking a balance and communicating in a way which may involve using the appropriate rules of grammar. One strategy that may help with this practice in therapy is the process of agenda setting. Irving Yalom, a prolific writer and therapist, has created videos of group psychotherapy situations in which he begins his group sessions with agenda setting for each client by letting them set the stage for what they would like to accomplish. This agenda setting focuses the discussion and provides structure and order. This process may require some redirection. The situation analysis (discussed above in the case of John) may assist with this maxim as well because it requires an orderly discussion of a situation with intentionality to separate actual events from interpretations of those said events and outcomes of the events.

COUNSELING SKILLS AND EMPATHIC SUCCESS

Counseling skills and techniques can also be used to help a client develop their story. Empathy is one of the most important of the skills (Nebrowsky, 2006; Sibcy, Warren, Knight, in press), as it can be much easier to face difficult truths with a caring or empathic other, rather than alone. Exhibiting empathy can take many forms (paralanguage, minimal encouragers, and non-defensiveness). In situations where the client has great difficulty sharing their story, these may be times when it is important to increase your empathy. Remember the attachment injuries and psychological insults discussed previously may be associated with shame and loneliness that one hides even from oneself, or as Byron Katie puts it, lies to oneself. *"Attachment failures lead to unprocessed feelings of unregulated grief, which, without the empathic other, create unbearable states of aloneness that can only be regulated with defenses"* (Nebrosky, 2006, p. 527; Sibcy & Knight, 2013).

Empathic counseling skills such as the basic listening sequence including reflecting content, reflecting feeling, and reflecting meaning may help a client clarify and make sense of their story in the context of a safe environment with a supportive other. Thompson (2010) talks about how in the Garden of Eden, Adam and Eve covered themselves with the fig leaf due to shame that was associated with sin. Shame is associated with covering or hiding, as in the case of the fig leaf, and perhaps in the case of the incoherent narrative. Thus the volume of empathy should be measured in order to help facilitate a safe environment where the client can face the shame with the empathic care of the counselor rather than alone. This is reminiscent of the old Swedish Proverb that says, "Shared joy is a double joy; shared sorrow is a halved sorrow." Recall that if the offending attachment injuries have been referred to as "empathic failures" in keeping with this conceptualization, how much more important is it to then make therapy an emphatic success? Cassidy, a prominent attachment researcher who has co-authored articles with Mary Main, in her publication, the *Handbook of Attachment*, stated, "Attachment theory encourages a therapist to reach, with empathic questions, reflections, and conjectures, behind partners and family members' masks and unpack separation distress, anger about rejections and hurts, and the attachment longings that color emotional reactions" (Cassidy & Shaver, 2016, p. 805). *Thus it is important to use high doses of cognitive and emotional empathy to search for the attachment longings and experiences that underlie the present moment.*

In therapy, when we are looking for changes in depressive symptomatology, relationship problems, etc., we may also seek to see an increase or valuing of attachment because valuing is a secure characteristic. What does it mean to value? Typically, we see that the client prizes or cherishes relationships with attachment figures and considers them important. Here, early messages could perhaps be decoded through some borrowed interventions from CBASP such as the Significant Other History (or SOH for short; where clients discuss about six key figures that have had a significant impact on them) or a Transference Hypothesis, in which a client identifies the imprint that early attachment figures have left on him or herself. This may help uncover some underlying beliefs and messages about the relationship. If the therapist engages in challenging interpersonal sameness through disciplined interpersonal involvement, then they can distinguish between hurtful messages from attachment figures in the past and messages from the therapist.

EMPATHY AND THE COUNSELOR

Given the role of empathic failure and the idea that abuse, neglect, and unloving experiences are considered to be the result of empathic failure, it is critical for the therapist to use a high dose of empathy. We may postulate that this is a primary healing function of therapy.

CAVEATS

"Wait a minute! I'm feeling like a lost ball in high weeds."

—*Gary Sibcy*

(A response to a client who gave an interpretation, when asked for a situation during situation analysis)

Congruence

Sometimes, when a client's story is not congruent or does not make sense, we begin to feel like the opening quote depicts, "A lost ball in high weeds." Early family therapy researchers noticed an increase in symptoms associated with schizophrenia after family visitation day at the hospital. This may sound somewhat surprising because of all of the literature indicating that family support is a resource for resilience. However, when communication patterns were observed, family members exhibited some communication patterns that could be characterized as double bind. This means that there was a mixed message embedded in the communication. It was as if a family member was sending the message, "go away" and "come close" at the same time. Therefore, double bind communication is sometimes referred to as crazy making behavior, as some would say "you're darned if you do and darned if you don't." For this reason, it is very important for clinicians to seek to communicate in a congruent way where there are not conflicting double bind messages. For example, using SOLER (which represents sitting in a position that is squarely facing the client, sitting with open posture, learning in, making steady eye contact, and reaming relaxed) nonverbal communication can ensure that a clinician is communicating a congruent message (open and interested) with respect to hearing the client story. This helps ensure that verbal and nonverbal communications align and are congruent in therapy, which may be healing for someone who has experienced many double binds.

CHAPTER 7 SUMMARY

Personal stories facilitate people's narratives. If a person's story "makes sense", it is congruent, coherent, and collaborative and is a hallmark of the secure autonomous attachment style. Earned secure speakers will have a coherent personal narrative even though they may have experienced adverse childhood experiences. There are a number of skills needed for someone to facilitate a coherent narrative, among the most important being empathy and mindfulness towards the speaker. Therapists are looking for an increase or valuing of attachment because it is a secure characteristic.

CHAPTER 8

Earned Secure:
Redeeming the Story

"The human psyche, like human bones, is strongly inclined towards self-healing."

—John Bowlby

The Earned Secure Attachment Status is an illustration of the power of redemption because an adult could have had developmental experiences associated with psychological insults and low grade trauma, yet still go on to develop a secure attachment style. The idea that someone is on a pathway to a disorganized attachment style and will maintain that relationship for life is an "outmoded concept and one most psychologists [and counselors] have rejected" (Marvin, 2016). Through other positive attachment relationships, establishing a coherent narrative, or "making sense of early attachment experiences" is more important than the experiences themselves. One could have a challenging early part of life with respect to attachment and still have opportunity for movement back to a secure autonomous pathway in later life.

One of the challenges in facilitating a change from moving away to moving towards (dismissing attachment onto the pathway to secure autonomous attachment), or getting tangled up in, to moving towards attachment in a free and clear way is the idea that these attachment related orientations often serve a regulatory function both emotionally and physiologically. For example, we heard Dr. James Coan, a professor at the University of Virginia in Charlottesville, VA speak at the International Attachment Conference in New York a few years ago, and he also authored a chapter in Cassidy and Shaver's *Handbook of Attachment* (2016), entitled "Towards a Neuroscience of Attachment" (Coan, p. 242) discusses how proximity seeking serves a regulatory function. For example, if a child is distressed he or she may seek closeness with his mother to regulate that distress, and this is characteristic of a secure autonomous attachment style. That caring and responsive caregiver helps to alleviate the child's sense of tension and anxiety. However, some researchers have suggested that the avoidance that is associated with a dismissing attachment style may also serve to regulate emotion (Cassidy & Shaver, 2016; Fraley, 1998). Thus, the avoidance is reinforced and this may make it more challenging for one who is high in avoidance to move towards a secure attachment.

FACING THE TRUTH

"If it's true it's true."

—John Bowlby

Moving towards a secure attachment style, also involves telling yourself the truth. Sometimes facing the truth of our story is difficult and painful, but it is a necessary work. Here is a case where the truth will set you free. John Bowlby (Bowlby, 1984) emphasized that it is of utmost importance to help clients explore their past. However, he also recognized and acknowledged that for many clients this is no easy feat. Especially if you grew up experiencing rejection or unloving behavior by a parent. In a video recorded by Lifespan Learning Institute, Bowlby talked about this dilemma, and indicated that even though it may be very difficult perhaps because it is too painful for a person to think about being unwanted or rejected by parents. However, Bowlby shares "yet if it's true, it's true; and they are going to be better off in the future if they recognized that that is what did happen (Bowlby, 1984, 1:10–1:19)."

Recall in the opening chapter we discussed "The Case for Grace" and found that Grace had loving experiences with her Grandmother. She valued the relationship, she missed her grandmother dearly after she passed away, and she still remembers her Grandmother fondly and values all that her Grandmother taught her. These are all characteristics of a secure autonomous speaker's transcript or attachment story. However, despite her loving experiences with her Grandmother, Grace also had to come to terms with the loss of an attachment figure.

REVIEW

In Chapter two we discussed the four primary attachment styles. Recall they include secure (freely moving towards a discussion of attachment experiences), dismissing (a turning away from attachment experiences), preoccupied (which typically involves getting tangled up in a discussion of attachment), and unresolved (an incoherent accounting of loss or abuse experiences).

However in addition to these four primary attachment styles, there is one more that has not been discussed quite as much. This 5th one is often referred to as "**earned secure**" which I think of as the "but God" classification or an example of redemption in the context of attachment. Recall from (Chapter 2: "Attachment Styles and Relationship Dynamics") earlier in the text that an earned secure attachment style is associated with an unloving childhood or a childhood experience where loving experiences are ranked 3 or less on the loving scale. Their early attachment figures may have fed and clothed them, but special warmth and affection and moderately loving experiences were sparse, if at all. However, despite this harsh background, speakers with this attachment style have managed to develop a coherent narrative and tell their story in a way that makes sense.

In Dan Siegel's language we might say they have "made sense" (2009) of their attachment relationship. In Curt Thompson's language from "Anatomy of the Soul", (2010) we may say that they have been vulnerable and come to know themselves and their attachment figures in a way that doesn't require hiding and shame.

In keeping with Thompson's description of the role of shame, a Judeo-Christian worldview perspective, the incoherence of an insecure or unresolved narrative actually comes from hiding the shame that is associated with early attachment experiences that were perhaps in the form of high grade or low grade trauma. *The counselor's role is very important in helping the client to face the truth of his or her story with an empathic other to buffer the loneliness and the pain.* To face the truth of one's story and to look unwavering into the pain of experiences perhaps in the form of rejection, neglect, physical abuse, sexual abuse, abuse from a caregiver, as well as acknowledging the fallen nature of humanity can feel like openly and willingly exposing oneself to the pain that cuts with the sharpness of a switch blade. To do this coherently requires one to refrain from flinching in the form of incoherence, such as becoming exaggerative, denying pain, or becoming overwhelmed by it. Rethinking back mentally, to the scene of the empathic failure of a loved one, this failure could perhaps perpetuate empathic failure in the self. The perpetuated empathic failure could be in the form of failure to forgive or the failure to look beyond, especially beyond the pain and to consider the deep pain and woundedness of the one inflicting the injury. How wounded must the attachment figure be that abuses his or her child? Or, how wounded must the attachment figure be who failed to protect the child from abuse (abuse the child, or who hurled harsh words like it was a game of darts)? How likely is it that the offending attachment figure experienced similar pain in his or her childhood and perpetuated it? In counseling we often refer to this as "intergenerational transmission" in lay terms perhaps "the sins of the fathers passed down to the next generation." However, thinking from the speaker's' perspective (the adult describing their attachment experiences now looking back on childhood) requires mindsight (mindsight may also be referred to as metacognitive monitoring or perspective taking) this a thinking beyond one's own experience to seek to connect with the state of mind of the other.

NEUROSCIENCE AND DISORGANIZED ATTACHMENT

The neuroscience literature (Sibcy & Knight, 2011; Thompson, 2010) discuss this idea that when we feel threatened we "lose our mind" and rather than thinking with our brain's CEO (Amen, 2011) the PFC and the brain stem or reptilian brain, the fight or flight response is activated and the capacity to make goal directed decisions and to think empathically may be temporarily offline (as the Amen clinics indicate empathy is a PFC function).

THE NEUROSCIENCE OF EMPATHY/EARNED SECURITY

Dr. Julie Gottman talks about how in her research with her husband John Gottman, they found that sometimes the anger in a person becomes so magnified that it is difficult to manage, and in the anger there is a desire to hurt the other person. Dr. Julie Gottman shared in an interview with

Dr. Tim Clinton (2013), that in these situations a person is often flooded. During flooding, the Gottmans found that heart rates were getting up to over 100 beats per minute (to put in perspective, according to my FitBit, as I am writing this paragraph my heart beat is at 79). Dr. Julie Gottman suggests that at this point it is time for people to recognize and say that it is time for a break! The twenty minutes may allow just enough time for the empathic shift, for a person to go from an angry state perceiving the other person as threatening to truly listening and seeking to take the other person's perspective (Gottman, 2013). This is part of the reason our roles as therapists are so important! We can help a person recognize the signs that they are becoming physiologically flooded by checking in with them as they tell their story, and recognizing the preoccupying anger that can be associated with flooding, and that is not conducive to developing empathy.

When a person tells their story, it requires neural integration to form sentences to put together ideas and words (Siegel, 2009) while also engaging the limbic system where emotional memories may be stored. These traumatic memories that have not been discussed may not have been activated while the language centers of the brain were activated. Neural integration involves the capacity for open communication, where various neurons are firing together and engaging at the same time. *The empathic other, the counselor, may provide a level of empathy in combination with the research based skills, that allows a speaker with an insecure attachment style (who is the survivor of many attachment injuries) the courage to face the truth of his or her story and now experience empathy in a situation where empathic failure once occurred.* The facilitation of perceived safety is part of the CBASP model and consistent with a Rogerian approach to counseling as well. A comprehensive discussion on the neurobiology of attachment is beyond this text, for more information consider Dr. Thompson's book, "The Anatomy of the Soul" (2010) or one of Dr. Amen's books revealing much about neuroscience in understandable terms.

EMPATHIC FAILURES

In the previous edition of the Diagnostic Statistical Manual of Mental Disorders IV, there were five axis for diagnosing psychopathology. The second axis represented personality disorders and these diagnoses were often considered by practitioners to be some of the more challenging cases to work with. I have heard from faculty and clinicians alike that Axis II diagnoses (personality disorders) are thought to be more resistant from treatment or more challenging to work with. However, attachment theory and the subsequent research on the Strange Situation, reveals much about the longings that may underlie some forms of psychopathology such as personality disorders.

In an article by Dr. Jeffrey Guira entitled *"The Talking Cure of Avoidant Personality Disorder: Remission the Earned-Secure Attachment"* (2016), Dr. Guina uses language that communicates something critically important! Dr. Guina shares that personality disorders were thought to be associated with negative experiences during childhood, but what struck me was the wording that Guina used to describe these experiences. He said, *"Personality disorders are commonly associated with negative experiences such as abuse, neglect, and other **empathic failures.**"* You have seen this phrase used in other portions of this text, and the definition is intuitive (a failure to be empathic), but let's take a closer look.

Dr. Guina conceptualizes abuse and neglect as empathic failures or failures to show empathy! Guina shares the story of a client who experienced childhood trauma and was dismissing in her attachment relationships and diagnosed with avoidant personality disorder. However, despite her difficult early experiences, over the course of psychotherapy, she was able to move to a secure autonomous attachment style! This movement from an insecure to a secure attachment is illustrative of the redemptive possibilities for healing attachment, and the hope that we can convey for those who wish for the latter part of life to be better than the former. So, in the remaining pages we turn our attention to facilitating growth. This is reminiscent of the words of Bobby Burns, the Plowman poet, who was a Scottish poet. Burns wrote, "The Best is Yet to Be." I recall from an English course long ago. *"The Best Is Yet to Be" captures the essence of the therapeutic factor, instillation of hope, and the idea that there is an empathic other to grow and face challenges with*:

"Grow old along with me!
The best is yet to be,
The last of life, for which the first was made:
Our times are in His hand
Who saith "A whole I planned,
Youth shows but half; trust God: see all, nor be afraid!"

CHAPTER 8 SUMMARY

A phrase, "empathic failure" is found in the literature to describe the phenomenon that occurs when an attachment figure abuses, neglects, or otherwise inflicts a psychological insult or attachment injury. It can be very painful or difficult to acknowledge the reality of these injuries, and yet in the words of John Bowlby, the Father of Attachment, "if it's true, it's true" and a person is better off facing the truth, despite the pain involved. This is a necessary struggle in being able to tell one's story in a coherent way and in facilitating movement towards an integrated secure attachment style. The activation of the pre-frontal cortex in constructing the story while also activating the limbic systems and areas where emotional memories are stored can lead to neural integration and adaptation, according to Dan Siegel and other prominent attachment writers and researchers.

Part III

Strategies for Growth

CHAPTER 9

Two Pathways for Seeking Proximity to the Divine Attachment Figure

"You can't go back and change the beginning,
but you can start where you are and change the ending."

—*C.S. Lewis*

ATTACHMENT AND FAITH/RELATIONSHIP TO GOD (PATHWAYS TO GOD ATTACHMENT)

In chapter four, we discussed how psychological insults from attachment figures or attachment injuries can be associated with other problems like chronic depression, and how God can be identified as an attachment figure based on the four requirements of an attachment figure (relationship, safe haven, secure base, separation anxiety/pain with loss). We also discussed the idea that there are different hypotheses regarding the pathways to attaching to God. We will discuss these pathways in more detail in this chapter.

Two pathways have been described to religion. This language is used in the literature and brings forth images of the Robert Frost poem, "The Road Not Taken." Consider the words of the poem:

> "Two roads diverged in a yellow wood,
> And sorry I could not travel both
> and be one traveler, long I stood.
> And looked down one as far as I could
> To where it bet in the undergrowth;
> Then took the other as just as fair,
> And having perhaps the better claim,
> Because it was grassy and wanted wear;
> Though as for the passing there
> had really worn them about the same.
>
> And both that morning equally lay
> In leaves no step had trodden black.
> Oh, I kept the first for another day!
> Yet knowing how way leads on to way,
> I doubted if I should ever come back.
>
> I shall be telling this with a sigh
> Somewhere ages and ages hence:
> Two roads diverged in a wood, and I—
> I took the one less traveled by,
> And that has made all the difference."

As Robert Frost so eloquently says, once we get accustomed to following a certain path, it may be doubtful that we would ever make a change. However, counselors are in the changing business and redemption is possible. Let's look at the two pathways.

PATHWAY #1

One path described in the literature may start with a child born into a family with sufficiently sensitive parents that are (mostly) religious (G, These names need to be spelled out. B, & H, 2014, p. 727). The child's subsequent relationship with God, the Heavenly Father, tends to mirror their relationship with their parents. In the literature, this is described as the social correspondence hypothesis (Granquvist and Kirkpatrick, 2008). This leads to a conceptualization of the Heavenly Father as one who is loving, and in addition, like the sensitive care giver, as one who is also accessible (Granquvist & Kirkpatrick, 2008). The relationship rules, that an individual has in this situation typically indicate that the self is worthy of love and others/ (including God) can be seen as reliable security providers.

PATHWAY #2: COMPENSATION OR REDEMPTIVE ATTACHMENT

*"What feels like the end of the world, is often only the beginning,
said the butterfly to the caterpillar."*

—Anita Knight

This is my personal favorite because it speaks of God's redemptive nature and of the way He can make all things new! We can see many examples of redeeming pain and positive change: from the caterpillar to butterfly, to the spring flower that emerges after the winter snow, to the sun peeking over the horizon of a pink and crimson sky after the dark night, He is the God of new beginnings and second chances. He does new things, and He is Jehovah-Rapha, the Robert Frost's poem, discussed earlier, depicts well the fact that there are choices in life and different paths that we can take and decision points. This second pathway regarding attachment and faith seems more intentional and perhaps the harder road. However, it may seem that the choice point may not be which pathway to take. One may think he or she is at the mercy of those who came before, so the choice, instead, may be how far to progress down this path, but when to change paths. Dr. Bob Marvin (2009) explains attachment as a set of unfolding pathways, and even if one has an insecure style or is unresolved for trauma, "life does offer second chances" and another pathway or attachment figure is likely to emerge. Some Psalms discuss the spiritual principle of making a changes despite previous generations or ancestors perpetuation of mistakes. Consider the words of Psalm 78 (ISV):

> "He established a decree in Jacob, and established the Law in Israel, that he commanded our ancestors to reveal to their children in order that the next generation—children yet to be born—will know them and in turn teach them to their children. Then they will put their trust in God and they will not forget his awesome deeds. Instead, they will keep his commandments. They will not be like the rebellious generation of their ancestors, a rebellious generation, whose heart was not steadfast, and whose spirits were unfaithful to God. The descendants of Ephraim were sharp shooters with the bow, but they retreated in the day of battle. They did not keep God's covenant, and refused to live by his Law. They have forgotten what he has done, his awesome deeds that they witnessed."

This pathway has been described in the literature as a path that relies on God as a Father, and even as what has been referred to as a surrogate attachment figure to regulate feelings of distress. This has been described in the literature as the compensation hypothesis. The warmth and sensitive availability of one's relationship with God is thought to have a compensatory effect on one's attachment based relationship rules.

Interestingly, even though these individuals may not grow up in a religious household or with parents that are religious, they are often very relational. It is not actually a parent's religiosity that predicts a child's perceived closeness to God, but instead it is the parent's sensitivity and availability to the child. So perhaps St. Francis of Assisi sensed this intuitively when stating, "Preach the gospel at all times. Use words only when necessary."

ATTACHMENT AND LOSS

"It is better to have loved and lost than never to have loved at all."

—Alfred Lord Tennyson

We quote Tennyson often, (as in the introduction to this section) because it is important to tell ourselves the truth when it comes to attachment, despite the difficulty involved. Inherent in valuing is loss. If we feel loss, then that is an indicator that we valued the person we lost. In the previous chapter we discussed the link between attachment and depression. Of course, loss may also be an impetus for feelings of sadness and depression. Attachment and emotion are closely linked. Since early childhood, babies seek proximity to their caregiver, and this seeking of nearness serves to help regulate heightened levels of arousal or emotional distress. Therefore, nearness to a sensitive attachment figure can be inherently comforting.

Grief and loss are some of the painful emotional experiences that are associated with the ending of an attachment relationship. John Bowlby, the Father of Attachment Theory, described some attachment processes that evoke emotional experiences in terms of how they manifest in relationships. He said:

> "Many of the most intense emotions arise around the formation of, the maintenance of, and the disruption and renewal of attachment relationships. The formation of a bond is described as falling in love, maintaining a bond as loving someone, and losing a partner as grieving over someone" (1979, p. 130).

Bowlby's words make sense as we consider the regulatory function that attachment plays and the transient nature of earthly attachment. Consider the scripture found in the book of Jeremiah Chapter 17: 5 (NIV), "Cursed is the man who trusts in mankind, who draws strength from mere flesh and whose heart turns away from the Lord . . . but blessed is the man who trusts in the Lord, whose confidence is in Him." *The loss experience is inevitable, and the grief that comes with loss is evidence of the love and value we had for our loved ones.*

Recall, Grace's Grandmother introduced her to what is often discussed in the literature as a "Divine Attachment Figure" (DAF) (Counted, 2016, p. 240).

John Bowlby (1999) shared that loss is an inherently disorganizing experience that requires a person to make changes to their outer world that are in line with their interiority. This can be a tough process and can result in people with a secure attachment style becoming disorganized when they lose an important figure in their life. However, attachment is fluid in both directions. A person can move from insecure or unresolved to secure or earned secure. However, a person can also move from secure to unresolved or insecure. Thus, an attachment shift can likewise be positive and, perhaps refer to an individual who grew up with lots of experiences of rejection and developed an avoidant attachment style, who sees the replacement attachment figure, or the person that will be loving and available to them and develops that relationship characterized by valuing and availability. Bob Marvin shared that early attachment relationships do not determine a person's destiny, and this idea that the past determines the future is an outmoded concept. Marvin insists that this is also a subject rejected by most psychologists (Marvin, personal communication, 2013). Change is possible, and as a helping professional, I am in the business of change. Although we know that change is difficult, we also know that change in a positive direction with intentionality is possible.

In this text, we will explore connecting with God as our Ultimate Divine Attachment figure and moving towards a secure autonomous attachment style. Since God has placed eternity in our hearts, each loss of a relationship is difficult. It reminds us of the temporal nature of humanity. We long for something lasting, and by lasting we refer to not only lifelong relationship, but even something that spans beyond the confines of this temporal life. In subsequent chapters, we will explore how the Divine Attachment Figure (DAF), God, offers many of the same relational qualities as other attachment figures and how some have found their relationship with God can be a healing factor (Compensatory) in early relationships.

CHAPTER 9 SUMMARY

The research on attachment reveals that there is a connection between the way a person experiences primary caregivers/attachment figures and attachment to God. This can be adaptive or maladaptive. There are several pathways. One is referred to in the research literature as the correlational hypothesis, which suggests there is a correlation between relationships with primary attachment figures and God attachment. If one has had warm and sensitive caregivers, then this can be positive. However, if a person has had experiences that would be considered unloving, harsh, neglectful or even abusive, then it can be hard to see God as a loving Father. This is where healing needs to take place, and the process of looking at a different pathway, such as the compensation pathway. This other is called the compensation hypothesis which suggests that if one has an experience of unloving relationships with primary care givers, then a warm relationship with God can compensate for some of these early attachment injuries. Although, a person may not be able to select the path they find themselves on originally, at some point there will be a decision point and there will be an opportunity to challenge thoughts about who God is and move towards embracing a more loving God image, and healing. This requires recognizing when attachment figures may have misrepresented what a loving Father would be like. Future chapters will discuss strategies for enhancing closeness/seeking proximity to the Heavenly Father and Heavenly or Divine Attachment Figure.

Attachment and loss is also discussed, and the idea that loss, though painful indicates to us that we valued a relationship and that it was important to us. Loss can be a disorganizing experience, but making sense of loss just like other experiences is important and can lead to resolution and a journey back to the path of secure attachment.

CHAPTER 10

Seeking Proximity to the Divine Attachment Figure

"'You will seek me and find me when you seek me with all your heart.
I will be found by you,' declares the Lord, 'and will bring you back from captivity.
I will gather you from all the nations and places where I have banished you," declares the
Lord, 'and will bring you back to the place from which I carried you into exile.'"

—*Jeremiah 29:13-15*

In previous chapters, we discussed how there are five different attachment styles including: dismissing, preoccupied, secure autonomous (continuous), unresolved, and earned secure. These attachment styles emerge from a combination of early childhood experiences with caregivers and state of mind with respect to those experiences. We also discussed children's attempt to connect with their caregivers, and the subsequent development of various attachment strategies that develop in the wake of those experiences. When attachment figures are unavailable (for whatever reason) often a state of unbearable aloneness that evoke defense mechanisms to help regulate the emotions of grief that are associated with these empathic failures (Nebrosky, 2006; Sibcy & Knight, 2011).

Although during adulthood, the attachment system orients from caregivers to romantic attachment figures, there may be instances, especially during difficult times, when one seeks closeness or proximity to a partner and that secure base/safe haven is unavailable. Researchers have found that during the Strange Situation proximity seeking serves a regulatory function. In other words, children protest their parent's departure because of the fear that it brings, and seek to reunite with them/protest their departure. This implies seeking closeness to an attachment figure during times of distress may help bring comfort and warmth (however, if the attachment figure is also the source of pain, rather than just comfort this emotion regulation strategy may backfire) and help regulate those feelings of distress.

There is one attachment figure that is always available, and that is where God, as an attachment figure, we speculate (and some research supports) may provide a healing effect and a pathway to a secure autonomous status or an earned secure attachment status.

Researchers have also assessed relationship with God from an attachment framework. Some of the key players in attachment research include Kirkpatrick from William and Mary and Granqist from the University of Stockholm. Granqvist and Kirkpatrick note (2016) that it is important not to extend attachment theory beyond its appropriate scope. Therefore, we need to ensure as we conceptualize God as an attachment figure and examine our relationship with Him in light of attachment dynamics, that we satisfy the requirements set forth in the literature to consider Him an attachment figure.

Some of the requirements of conceptualizing one as an attachment figure include first that a relationship must exist, because after all an attachment is first and foremost a relationship. Granqvist and Kirkpatrick (2016) report that when asked in a Gallup poll (Gallup & Jones, 1989) that asked, "Which of the following four statements comes closest to your own view of 'faith':

1. A set of beliefs

2. Membership in a church or synagogue

3. Finding meaning in life

4. Relationship with God?"

Most people responded that their view of faith involved a "relationship with God." Now that the relationship characterization is established, next let's look at the four requirements for an attachment figure (or attachment relationship).

These four requirements for one to relate to God as an attachment figure are as follows: 1) maintenance of proximity, 2) conceptualizing God as a secure base, 3) Conceptualizing God/ the attachment figure as a safe haven, and 4) separation anxiety that is activated upon separation or death (Ainsworth, 1985). This comes from Mary Ainsworth (recall Ainsworth worked with John Bowlby). We will explore each of these four requirements in more detail and will discuss each of these aspects of relationship with God in more detail (as well as look at how God meets these criteria).

Beck and McDonald (2004) wrote an article in the Journal of Psychology and Theology called, "*Attachment to God: The Attachment to God Inventory*: *tests of working model correspondence and an exploration of faith group differences*." The same patterns are described in reference to relationship with God and may be measured relative to levels of anxiety and avoidance. Recall, that since attachment behaviors are designed to regulate emotion, attachment styles tend to be indicative of levels of anxiety or avoidance (avoidance is a mechanism to deactivate attachment related anxiety), a disorganized attachment style can sometimes be indicated by a preoccupation with fearful or traumatic experiences and exhibit a combination of anxious and avoidant attachment behaviors (Beck and & McDonald, 2004, as cited in Counted, 2016).

Although we cannot put God in a box, as Foster says in his text, "Celebration of Discipline" (2003), "an unsuspected grace that God refuses to be a puppet on our strings or a genie in our bottle . . .". In the literature, God has been written about as a "substitute attachment figure" (Counted, 2016,

p. 317), and it is conceptualized that over time as the relationship with God grows and becomes stronger, God becomes a dominant attachment figure. God is the Father of all attachment figures (no pun intended) from a Judeo-Christian perspective. *Some may argue that rather than God being a "substitute attachment figure" He is the ultimate attachment figure, and others are substitutes that may have misrepresented him due to the fallen nature of creation.* From a Judeo-Christian worldview, Jesus directs us to address God and call God, "our Father."

Let's zoom out for a moment and look at a biblically based conceptualization. I went to graduate school at Regent University in Virginia Beach. I found out that a Regent is one who stands in for the King. Yeshua, Yahweh, Almighty God is the King of Kings and the Lord of Lords! As a Christ follower, the King of Kings, Almighty God, is your Father. You are a child of the most-high God. The Bible says, "though my father and mother forsake me, the Lord will take me up" (Psalm 27:10; NASB), another version the Holman Christian Standard Bible says it this way, "Even if my father and mother abandon me, the LORD cares for me." This is something to meditate on, and we will come back to this later in this text.

Recall, previously, we discussed that the attachment figure needs to serve as a **safe haven** during times of distress and a secure base as a place to launch from for exploration. The person must also be able to seek proximity towards the attachment figure and must also suffer some discomfort or anxiety during times of separation. Let's look at how God meets and surpasses these requirements. Let's look at some bullet points relevant to seeking God as our Haven of Safety.

RELATING TO GOD AS OUR SAFE HAVEN

- ✓ Recall children need to be able to seek their parents when their battery power is low and they need to "recharge" so to speak.

- ✓ They need open arms/hands during times of distress; adults also need a safe place to turn to recharge.

- ✓ In a study conducted on 7–12-year-olds in Finland, Taminen (1994) reported children felt closer to God during times of distress especially in times of:
  - ✗ Emergency and
  - ✗ Loneliness

Psalm 91 uses imagery to express how God is our haven of safety.

Consider the passage:

> "Whoever dwells in the shelter of the Most High will rest in the shadow of the Almighty. I will say of the Lord, 'He is my refuge and my fortress, my God, in whom I trust.' Surely he will save you from the fowler's snare and from the deadly pestilence. He will cover you with his feathers, and under his wings you will find refuge; his faithfulness will be your shield and rampart. You will not fear the terror of night, nor the arrow that flies by day, nor the pestilence that stalks in the darkness, nor the plague that destroys at midday. A thousand may fall at your side, ten thousand at your right hand, but it will not come near you. You will only observe with

your eyes and see the punishment of the wicked. If you say, 'The Lord is my refuge,' and you make the Most High your dwelling, no harm will overtake you, no disaster will come near your tent. For he will command his angels concerning you to guard you in all your ways; they will lift you up in their hands, so that you will not strike your foot against a stone. You will tread on the lion and the cobra; you will trample the great lion and the serpent. 'Because he loves me,' says the Lord, 'I will rescue him; I will protect him, for he acknowledges my name. He will call on me, and I will answer him; I will be with him in trouble, I will deliver him and honor him. With long life I will satisfy him and show him my salvation.'"

Contemplate these words, "I will say of the Lord He is my refuge and my fortress, my God in whom I trust." He is my safe haven. Consider the Psalmist who knew who his safe haven was, he said, "God is our refuge and strength, an ever present help in time of trouble." In 1 Samuel 13:14, David is called "a man after God's own heart" and He was also a man who found His safe haven and secure base in God.

GOD ATTACHMENT AND RELIGIOUS TRADITIONS

Some of the key players in the God-attachment research include Granqvist and Kirkpatrick. Pehr Granqvist is an attachment researcher at Stockholm University in their Department of Psychology. Much of Granqvist's teaching and research focuses on attachment and spirituality, and he did his doctoral dissertation on those constructs. Granqvist, in keeping with this line of research, wrote an article with two of his colleagues entitled, "Attachment, religiousness, and distress among the religious and spiritual: Links between religious syncretism and compensation" (Granqvist, Broberg, and Hagekull, 2014). The term syncretism is defined by Merriam-Webster as "the combination of different forms of belief or practice" (Merriam-Webster, nd, https://www.merriam-webster.com/dictionary/syncretism). In this article the researchers discuss a study where they examined three primary variables: 1) attachment, 2) distress and 3) religiousness among four groups. The four groups include: 1) the traditionally religious, 2) new age, 3) spiritual, and 4) religiously syncretistic (recall syncretistic involves the fusion of multiple religious philosophies). They had a sample size of 75 participants. They found that the group that identified as religiously syncretistic had a larger number of participants that demonstrated an insecure attachment style, and that these participants were often raised by non-religious parents. The authors deduced that their parents were somewhat insensitive. The religiously syncretic group expressed that they had a "personal relationship with God" (Granqvist, Broberg, & Hagekull, 2014, p. 726). This group also had exhibited surges in spirituality during dark and trying life circumstances. The group that identified as new agers were similar to the religiously syncretistic with an exception. The new age group did not include a larger number of insecurely attached participants and they did not report a personal relationship with God. However, this new age group did report increased distress. The group that identified as "traditionally religious" (Granqvist, Broberg, & Hagekul, 2014, p. 726) were comprised of participants that tended to be low on distress, raised by religious parents, and somewhat sensitive.

Granqvist and his colleagues took away from this the idea that people that identify as religiously syncretic may use religion to compensate. Their research also revealed a perceived relationship with God may decrease risk of distress among those that are at risk.

CHAPTER 11
Strategies for Enhancing Attachment Security

"Traumatized people live with seemingly unbearable sensations: They feel heartbroken and suffer from intolerable sensations in the pit of their stomach or tightness in their chest. Yet avoiding feeling these sensations in our bodies increases our vulnerability to being overwhelmed by them."

—*Bessel A. van der Kolk*, The Body Keeps the Score

Life is full of paradoxes. A paradox is defined as, "a statement that is seemingly contradictory or opposed to common sense and yet is perhaps true" (Merriam-Webster, n.d.). Sometimes stories seem paradoxical, and sometimes, there is pressure to tell a story in a socially acceptable way even when the truth is far from socially acceptable.

A PARADOX

In order to be an overcomer, one has to experience adversity to overcome. In order to have a testimony, one must experience a test. Many good movies involve a dilemma, conflict, or some form of obstacle that the protagonist must face or a villain that the protagonist must defeat. We do not despise a story or movie because there has been adversity. Yet, when telling our personal story there may be a sense of shame in terms of how to face the difficulties, give words, or name them and talk honestly about deeply painful experiences. There may even be a sense that a person has to have positive experiences in childhood in order to have a secure attachment style; however, this is not true because in order to have a secure autonomous attachment style, a person must be able to speak of their negative experiences coherently. Despite this, there still may be this desire in a person to present a socially acceptable or pleasing story rather than the sometimes painful reality. We often refer to this as "social desirability bias." However, the paradoxical truth here is that the pleasing answer is not necessarily the most pleasing in terms of attachment security, rather the consistent coherent truth is (despite the possibility that it may include trauma, loss, or other painful difficulties).

EMOTION REGULATION AND PARADOXICAL STORIES

In other words, a person with a secure attachment style is able to share their story, both the good and bad experiences, in an emotionally intelligent way. Let me clarify what this means by taking just a moment to define emotional intelligence. Please note, there are multiple schools of thought about what emotional intelligence (EI) is. Some researchers describe it as a set of self-reported traits (Petrides & Furnham, 2006). While other authors, such as Daniel Goleman, who explores the questions of what is going on when some people of high IQ, seem to struggle. He postulates that this is due to a set of dispositions or abilities that he refers to as EQ, which he believes includes (Goleman, 1994), self-control (also found in the trait based model), zeal (unique from the other models), and persistence (some may see this as linked to emotion regulation), and the ability to motivate oneself (this may also be associated with or a function of emotion regulation). Still other researchers, including John Mayer, Pater Salovey, and David Caruso define it as an ability similar to intelligence. There are some areas of overlap and some areas of distinction in these different perspectives on emotional intelligence. One distinction is that Mayer, Salovey, and Caruso evaluate EI in an ability-based (Knight, 2009) format similar to an achievement test while most of the other EI researchers use self-report to evaluate EI. Petrides indicates 15 traits that are part of the construct of emotional intelligence, these traits include the following (Petrides, 2007).

> "Adaptability: flexible and willing to adapt to new conditions
>
> Assertiveness: forthright, frank and willing to stand up for their rights
>
> Emotion perception (self and others): clear about their own and other people's feelings
>
> Emotion expression: capable of communicating their feelings to others
>
> Emotion management (others): capable of influencing other people's feelings
>
> Emotion regulation: capable of controlling their (own) emotions
>
> Impulsiveness (low): reflective and less likely to give in to their urges
>
> Relationships: capable of having fulfilling personal relationships
>
> Self-esteem: successful and self-confident
>
> Self-motivation: driven and unlikely to give up in the face of adversity
>
> Social awareness: accomplished networkers with excellent social skills

Stress management: capable of withstanding pressure and regulating stress

Trait empathy: capable of taking someone else's perspective

Trait happiness: cheerful and satisfied with their lives

Trait optimism: confident and likely to 'look on the bright side' of life"

Both Petrides in his research (trait based) and Mayer, Salovey and Caruso in their research, look at **emotion regulation** as an important construct. Since a full discussion of EI is beyond the scope of this text, we will look at the sub-skill of **emotion regulation**, in terms of what both sets of researchers have to offer. Ability-based emotional intelligence is broken down into four capacities that are as follows: 1) the ability to identify emotions in facial expressions, 2) the ability to facilitate thought, 3) the ability to understand emotional information, and 4) the ability to regulate emotions in the self and others. Each of these four branches includes other tasks, and they are hierarchical, meaning that in order to engage in the task of regulating emotions, we must be able to first identify emotion, use emotions to facilitate thought, and have the capacity to understand emotional information.

The fourth branch of EI, the capacity to regulate emotions in the self and others involves several other tasks includes:

1. the capacity to remain open to a range of feelings that include both pleasant feelings and unpleasant feelings,

2. the ability to effectively engage with a feeling or detach from that feeling based on utility,

3. the capacity to monitor emotions both in the self and in others, and

4. the capacity to moderate negative emotions in the self or others and to enhance positive emotions without exaggerating them (Mayer and Salovey, 2007; Sibcy & Knight, 2011).

In order to share one's attachment story (or early relationship history, as in the case of the AAI) we need to use these capacities. For example, if Grace is sharing her attachment history and gives an open, honest, free account of her experiences, this requires a capacity to remain open to a range of feelings both pleasant and unpleasant. She may feel grief or sorrow as she remembers her beloved Grandmother's passing or she may feel anger as she thinks of times she encountered psychological insults. She may also feel joy at memories related to connection and love. All of these experiences may be a part of her story, and if she cuts herself off from feeling sadness or anger or joy, then she may struggle to accurately give an account of her experiences.

Thus the literature on strategies for enhancing emotional intelligence, including the capacity to stay open to positive and negative feelings would be important for telling one's story as well as the capacity to determine whether or not to engage with a feeling based on the utility of that emotion. Research illustrates that the following strategies are found to be effective in helping enhancing this top tier of emotional intelligence the capacity to regulate emotions: music (Saarikallio, 2011), mindfulness (Hill & Updegraff, 2012; van Overveld, Mehta, Smidts, Figner, Lins, 2012,), cognitive strategies (Eippert et al., 2006), dialectical behavior therapy (Azizi et al., 2012), and biofeedback video games (Ducharme, 2012).

MUSIC

Music has been defined as one of the biggest forms of self-regulation (Saarikallio, 2011; Knight, Bruns, & Captari, 2013). In this section we will look at some research that reveals how people tend to use music to regulate and some thoughts on how to use this research to inform practice.

Suvi Saarikallio who works in the Department of Music at a University in Finland conducted a qualitative research study that involved interviewing 21 participants in the age range of 21–70 about the strategies they employed for emotional self-regulation. The results clarified different trends in self-regulation and that music was deployed as a strategy for regulating emotion.

Happy Mood Maintenance

One regulation strategy involved what the researcher called, "happy mood maintenance" (Saarikallio, 2011, p. 312). When participants used music to preserve a happy mood, they revealed that this took forms such as turning up the volume on the music, becoming actively involved with the music by singing along, playing along with a musical instrument, or dancing to the music. The most frequently used strategy in the study revealed the use of background music to create a nice atmosphere and ambiance. Participants revealed that music could be an experience to get actively involved with or it could enhance almost any other existing activity by helping either enhance a positive mood or maintain the existing positive mood. Here are some quotes from study participants at both ends of the age range (Saarikallio, 2011, p. 312):

> "'I really listen quite a lot while at home, while doing dishes, cleaning, and anything. It's nice to have some noise there. If you're doing something, it somehow goes with that.' (Kathryn, 21)
>
> 'When you listen to a song, you start to sing along, it sweeps you along . . . And if [at] that moment a happy song comes, you sing and dance along.' (Shirley, 70)"

Music for Promoting Relaxation

Other themes related to strategies that emerged for music to assist with mood management included "using music as a means of revival and relaxation" (Saarikallio, 2011, p. 312), meaning that participants reported that they may have laid down or sat in a relaxed position and used the music to revive themselves and give them new energy from listening to music, or they may have found that it helped them relax by listening to it before bed. One participant said:

> "'I used to come home from work, and then you sit on a rocking chair, lift your feet up on a chair, and there's good music, then after 10 minutes you feel as if half of your housekeeping work has already been done, even though it has not. (Ann, 63)." (Saarikallio, 2011, p. 312).

There were individual differences that stood out in the themes of the interviews. For example, Saarikallio (2011) reported that all of the research participants mentioned using music to do the mental processing of working through unsettling emotions. However, a few participants that were in their 60's that liked to play musical instruments reported that they used improvisation to complete this process. Other participants primarily listened to music. Saarikallio shared a participant, William, who recounted how music helped him, here is what William said about how he works through this process:

> "'There are people who actually nourish their pain. And perhaps you can somehow live through your pain while you hear someone sing sad songs . . . I've been thinking that I go through the feelings I have so that I don't try to force myself to feel better by listening to something happy while I'm sad . . . I think that for me it helps, that if I'm dealing with some problem, and if there is also some music that deals with it, it does help me . . . I believe the changes in harmony are such, when the chords progress, and certain evergreens, they bring so many associations, and somehow help you to work through . . . I clearly work through my feelings through the music. (William, 65)'" (Saarakillio, 2011, p. 314)

In addition to being used for happy mood maintenance and processing through difficult emotions, participants in the research study also took comfort in music and found solace in music. I could see themes related to attachment in what Sarakillio shared about how one of the participants reported on how music comforted her in the wake of the loss of her late husband. Nancy shared:

> "But after more time has passed, now, that song by Albinoni gives me a really peaceful and good feeling, and I almost smile, and think back through our life, and that I was given the chance to work through the loss for such a long time, together with him at the hospital, spent the night there and all, and his departure was so gentle and so, so that song makes me actually feel really good nowadays. I can't do anything else while I'm listening to it, I just listen, sit down, and think back, with gratitude, with love.' (Nancy, 69)" (2011, p. 314).

Nancy's narrative includes attachment language and indicates that she highly valued the relationship that she had with her lost loved one. She also expressed how the music brings her a sense of peace and gratitude.

In addition to Saarikillo's qualitative research revealing applications of music for self-regulation, there are others that have acknowledged benefits of music on mood and brain function. Neuroscientists such as Dr. Amen have also discussed (on his social media YouTube posts) that learning to play a musical instrument has a positive impact on brain function. Music therapists have used strategies such as drumming circles to have a therapeutic effect.

As Saarikillo's (2011) study reveals, there are some individual differences in the deployment of music for a regulation strategy, and also some common themes across qualitative interviews. It may be useful to ask clients if and how they use music to regulate their mood, as well as share psychoeducational information on how others have used music effectively to regulate. This is one strategy for helping client's to develop skills and strategies to increase their Emotional Intelligence, particularly the skill of emotion regulation. Perhaps the discussion of one's attachment history brings up some feelings of sorrow, shame, anxiety, or another uncomfortable emotion. Music can provide solace as it did for Nancy or help one work through the mental processing as it did for William. Anecdotally, I have found that music serves not only as a helpful emotional regulation tool, but also as a helpful tool for facilitating one's relationship story. I have asked my clients and supervisees to identify a "theme song" that may represent their current plight, dilemma, struggle, or learning experience. Sometimes when a musical artist sings about a painful situation, it has the power of normalizing it and destigmatizing the phenomenon, thus perhaps, helping an individual with a similar experience to tell his or her story. Initially, when a client comes in for therapy who has survived adverse childhood experiences, it may be difficult for them to discuss their experiences in a coherent manner, and to coherently and comfortably approach (rather than avoid or get overwhelmed by) the narration of their story. A therapeutic discussion of music for self-regulation may be helpful for clients who would be willing to use music both inside and outside of treatment for regulation activities such as regulating anxiety, promoting peace, and positive mood, etc.

MINDFULNESS

In addition to music serving a regulatory function, mindfulness practices may also be helpful in the regulation of emotion, recent trends also demonstrate the mindfulness may play a role in adaptive brain function. Mindfulness has been defined as, "cultivating awareness and acceptance of the present moment" (Roemer, Williston, and Rollins, 2015, p. 52). Mindfulness researchers have found that a primary impact that mindfulness has on a person's physiology is the association with healthy emotion regulation, which is said to include, "reduced intensity of distress, enhanced emotional recovery, reduced negative self-referential processing, and/or enhance in ability to engage in goal-directed behavior" (Roemer, Williston, and Rollins, 2005, p. 52). Researchers believe mindfulness practices may not only predict these positive outcomes in healthy emotion regulation, but also may be the cause of them. However, more research is needed to understand all of the mechanisms by which mindfulness influences emotion regulation and the other aforementioned positive associations.

Mindfulness can be a challenging state of mind to achieve. It is possible to fall into the trap of thinking about what could have been, should have been, or alternate paths. Ruminating, especially on negative thoughts or experiences from the past can be associated with depression. In addition to living in the past, another alternative to being mindful of the present moment is living in the future. Living in the future may involve worrying about things to come, excessive planning, or a number of other distractions from the present moment. To be here in the moment right now may truly be a challenge. However, from a Christian perspective, this is where we encounter God, in the present moment. When Moses asked the Lord who he should say sent him, the Lord told him to say, "I Am". Here is the passage from Exodus 3:14–15 (NIV):

> "God said to Moses, "I am who I am. This is what you are to say to the Israelites: 'I am has sent me to you.'"

God is the Great "I Am." He is here with us in the present moment. When we are present in this moment, we are not preoccupied with worries about the future. Matthew 6:34 says (NAS), "Therefore, do not be anxious for tomorrow, for tomorrow will care for itself. Each day has enough trouble of its own." Likewise, when we are here in this present moment, we are not burdened with past disappointments that could weigh us down. Biblically, we are encouraged not to ruminate on the past, but to stay mindful of God's presence with us in the present moment and to attend to the new things He is doing today. Isaiah 43:18–25 (Holman Christian Standard Bible) says:

> "Do not remember the past events,
> pay no attention to things of old.

Look, I am about to do something new;
even now it is coming. Do you not see it?"

Since much mindfulness practice came out of the Eastern traditions of Buddhism, some Christian clients may feel uncomfortable with mindfulness interventions (Garzon & Ford, 2016). Christian mindfulness research suggests that one way to address these concerns is to adapt mindfulness based interventions to make them more culturally sensitive. They provide two adaptations of mindfulness exercises including: 1) breathing meditation, and 2) loving kindness meditation. Garzon and Ford have adapted the two aforementioned mindfulness exercises so they are more congruent with the themes of a Christian worldview.

Garzon and Ford adapted the traditional breathing meditation and developed a script. It is very similar to the Contemplative Prayer Exercise. I appreciate the way they adapted the activity to focus on God and our relationship with Him as our Creator. Let's take a look at the breath meditation and the script they use. The script is as follows:

"I'd like you to make yourself comfortable, sitting in a relaxed posture, closing your eyes or finding a spot in the room to let your eyes focus on. Allow yourself to switch from the usual active or doing mode to a mode of simply being, of resting in God's caring presence. As you allow your body to become still, bring your attention to the fact that you are breathing. The breath is a reminder of God creating us, "And the Lord God formed man of the dust of the ground, and breathed into his nostrils the breath of life; and man became a living soul." [Gen. 2:7]. With every breath in, you can recognize God breathing His life into you. With every breath out you can place yourself in His hands, resting in the Lord. Breathe in His life, breathe out resting in Him. There is no need to change anything. Just breathe naturally. He is with you in your experience, giving you love and grace.

And now focus on your breath more intently. If your mind wanders into other things, this is normal. No need to criticize yourself. Simply release those thoughts into God's loving hands and return to your breath. There is no need for a long prayer, a simple yielding and turning of your focus back to the breath is releasing these things to God.

Become aware of the movement of your breath as it goes into your body and as it leaves your body. Notice how it feels to you. No need to manipulate the breath in any way or change it. Simply be aware of it and of any feelings associated with breathing. Observe how the air feels going into your nostrils . . . Perhaps you can feel the airflow inside your nostrils into your sinuses, and down into your lungs as you breathe in. Notice how the breath feels deep down in your belly. Observe the abdomen as it expands when you breathe in, and as it falls when you breathe out. Expanding and falling. Expanding and falling. Observe how the air feels going out . . . Be completely here in each moment with each breath. No need to try to do anything, no need to get any place, simply be with your breath.

Ride the waves of your breath, observing the rhythmic pattern. If your mind wanders, gently release those thoughts into God's hands and bring it back to the moment-to moment sense of the flow of your breathing . . . Your breath anchors your attention, bringing you back to the present moment whenever you notice that your mind is becoming absorbed or reactive to something. Just be with your breath.

In a moment, the breathing meditation will end. Whatever way you would like to end this time will be fine. And when you are ready, bring your awareness back to the room, opening your eyes" (Garzon & Ford, 2016, p. 263).

CHAPTER 11 SUMMARY

It may seem as if when recounting attachment memories we should just emphasize the good and present in a socially acceptable way. However, this is contrary to the truth. Remember, from previous chapters, it is important to recognize the truth of our experience, despite the fact that it may be harsh or unloving. One must be able to narrate experiences both positive and challenging in order to successfully develop a coherent narrative and a secure autonomous attachment style. In the case of those who have endured psychological insults in the form of low grade trauma or other painful attachment experiences, denying the truth or focusing on the good has the opposite effect. One must instead face the truth with courage and narrate his or her story in a coherent way in order to move towards attachment security. In stories fraught with painful experiences and psychological insults, this can be difficult and requires emotion regulation. There are several different schools of thought on emotional intelligence, but in this chapter we focused on Petrides model and Mayer Salovey, and Caruso's model both of which include emotion management/regulation. Strategies for increasing emotion regulation skills are provided including music (i.e. happy music for mood maintenance, music for solace, etc.), mindfulness (a Christian alternative is provided), and other activities.

CHAPTER 12
Strategies for Strengthening Attachment to God

"What comes into our minds when we think about God
is the most important thing about us."

— A. W. Tozer

As we discussed previously on pathways to God attachment, an attachment figure must meet several requirements. Granqvist and Kirkpatrick lay out three criteria (and Cassidy adds a fourth) for one to serve as an attachment figure which include: 1) He must be someone you can seek proximity to (through prayer, worship, etc.), 2) He must serve as a secure base, 3) He must serve as a safe haven, 3) Separation is associated with a sense of loss or anxiety. Cassidy (1999) added one more requirement, 4) which is the attachment figure must be seen as stronger and wiser. Let's look at strategies for enhancing one's relationship with God in these ways. Recall that the attachment behavioral system involves seeking out the attachment figure as a safe haven during times of distress and then launching out from the attachment secure base to explore the world around oneself. Consider Mark 3:13–14 (NIV) "Then He went up the mountain and summoned those He wanted, and they came to Him. He also appointed 12. He also named them apostles—to be with Him, to send them out to preach . . ." Notice, Jesus called them first to "be with Him" and then he sent them out. This reminds me of the "Circle of Security" and the attachment behavioral system (Marvin & Seagroves, 2016; Bowlby, 1975) in which the child seeks proximity to the attachment figure and then after "being with" the attachment figure, launches out to explore the environment. Jesus calls us to Himself and then sends us out into the world.

Dr. George Jefferson, a well-respected counselor-educator who served as a professor, supervisor, and mentor after 31 years (and my mentor, supervisor, and professor for several years during graduate school) at Regent/CBN University sent out an email sharing his news of retirement with colleagues and students. He reminded us of this very important concept in the poetic and comforting language that he was known for:

> "In my venerable old age, I remember the King James version: 'The lines are fallen unto me in pleasant places' Ps. 16:6. I have been thinking of retirement for some time. A few days after graduation several streams came together and I have finally retired. I rather like the new chapter in my life although I have read only the first pages. I am glad for my 31 years at CBN/Regent University. The best part of all this has been students and my colleagues. I thank all of you. I will ride off into the sunset and you will get on with God's call on your life. Always remember that Jesus "called them to be with Him" (Mark 3:13,14) before He sent them out. May the grace of our Lord Jesus Christ be with us all."

—Dr. Jefferson

Contributed by George Jefferson. © Kendall Hunt Publishing Company

PROXIMITY SEEKING

Part of an attachment relationship is the capacity to seek proximity. Since God has called us first to be with Him (See Mark 3:13–14 above), spending time with him nurturing the attachment relationship is important. This can take the form of traditional individual prayer, contemplative prayer, praise and worship, confession, corporate prayer, and corporate worship. Here are some strategies that have been used to seek proximity to God:

- ✓ Spiritual Disciplines (Foster, 2002);
- ✓ Foster discusses in his text, "Celebration of Discipline" the spiritual disciplines including:
- ✓ Inward disciplines
    - ✗ Mediation
    - ✗ Prayer
    - ✗ Fasting
    - ✗ Study
- ✓ Outward disciplines
    - ✗ Simplicity
    - ✗ Solitude
    - ✗ Submission Services
- ✓ Corporate disciplines
    - ✗ Worship

- ✘ Guidance

- ✘ Celebration

- ✔ Believers have a desire to be "close" to God which is an example of a desire for proximity (Kirkpatrick, 1999)

GOD AS A SAFE HAVEN

God has been referred to as a "Divine Attachment Figure" in the research on attachment (Counted, 2016) and also as a "symbolic attachment figure" (Cassiba, Granqvist, and Costantini, 2011, p. 52). When Cassiba and colleagues use the language of the "symbolic attachment figure," they distinguish God from other unseen attachment figures. Despite, the widespread belief in God and personal faith, in our fallen world and in our humanness, we long for a seen and tangible attachment figure to interact with, feel, touch, and connect with in a familiar way that is warm and soothing. In this, some Christians find that the disappointment or loneliness that occurs when we do not find that in human counterparts is actually a longing for heaven (Jefferson, personal communication). Ecclesiastes 3:11 is about the idea that God set eternity in the heart of man: It says, "He has made everything appropriate in its time. He has also set eternity in their heart, yet so that man will not find out the work which God has done from the beginning even to the end." (NASB).

The NIV, says:

> "He has made everything beautiful in its time. He has also set eternity in the human heart; yet no one can fathom what God has done from beginning to end."

I like the NLT translation that says:

> "Yet God has made everything beautiful in its time. He has planted eternity in the human heart, but even so, people cannot see the whole scope of God's work from beginning to end."

This Scripture is redemptive and it confirms the validity of the grieving process of the person with the secure autonomous attachment style. If God has placed eternity in our hearts, then we long for something lasting because every human relationship is temporal. Each one has its beginning and its end: the attachment figures may be divorced, may move away, or there may be a break in the relationship or one may leave and abandon the figure (Counted, 2016). These human relationships are temporary but relationships with God the Father can be eternal.

Counted (2016) researched fifteen Christian youth in South Africa and explored how they related to God as an attachment figure. Counted indicated that participants had a personal relationship with God that satisfied the criteria of them being able to relate to God and seek proximity to Him, find a safe haven in Him to retreat to during times of distress, a secure base in Him to launch from to explore the surrounding environment, a response during times of separation, and a sense that God is both stronger and wiser (Counted, 2016; Granqvist & Kirkpatrick, 2008). Participants varied in racial background and church identification. The study was of a qualitative nature in that Counted conducted interviews that were recorded, and subsequently transcribed, analyzed, and deconstructed. In the analysis, themes were uncovered (it is worth noting that Counted revealed that the fifteen participants were part of an earlier survey that was quantitative in nature and the participants were found to score high on the anxiety scale).

Language that may reveal attachment themes could emerge in the interviews as participants describe their experiences with God, and it was especially important for researchers to look for keywords that were indicative of relating to God as the one to obtain closeness and proximity with as a haven of safety to retreat to during times of distress, as a secure base to move out and explore the world from, as one from whom separation is painful, and as one who is stronger and wiser (Counted, 2016).

GOD IMAGE AND GOD CONCEPT

As we move to relating to God as an attachment figure, there first may be some prerequisite work in addressing our God image and God concept. God concept is a phrase that typically involves a cognitive understanding of God, where God image typically relates to an emotional experience of God. During my time studying at Regent University, one of my professors, Dr. Glenn Moriarity, was researching God concept and God image. During a psychopathology class, he asked us to take out a blank sheet of paper and on one side of the page he invited us to sketch a picture of us and God when things were going well. We took a few moments to do this.

Next, Dr. Moriarity (circa 2005, personal communication) asked us to flip the page over and draw a picture of you and God after you have sinned. There was a sobering silence that filled the room as we conjured up images in our mind's' eye. This was Dr. Moriarity's in-class assessment that evaluated God Image. He explained oftentimes people experience a distinction between their God image and God concept. In other words there is often a distinction between how we experience God emotionally and what we know about Him intellectually. Sometimes we refer to this as cognitive dissonance, or a lack of congruence, between thoughts and feelings. For example, if Shenequa knows God loves her intellectually, but does not feel loved by God emotionally then she may experience cognitive dissonance. Otherwise described as a discrepancy between God image and God concept. (For more on God Image, see the work of Glenn Moriarity).

Counted's use of "God attachment language" (Counted, 2016, p. 323) is similar to Moriarity's construct of God image. Counted looked for themes in interviews he conducted with respect to how participant's used God-attachment language, but also noticed how they discussed ideas related to their God concept. Counted (2016) discussed Lou's research with regard to the idea that a participant's vocabulary is significant. Participants use "vocabularies" (Counted, 2016, p. 323) to make sense of suffering.

One interesting concept here is that metaphors and symbolic language are said to reveal the degree of closeness an individual feels towards God in their personal relationship with Him. This reminds me of a book that is written by authors John Trent and Gary Smalley (1982) entitled, "The Blessing." In "The Blessing", Trent and Smalley discuss the idea that there are Biblical examples of a parent passing on their blessing to a child (Trent and Smalley also argue that a child can also give their parent the blessing). This reminds me of a quote I recently heard, *"The amazing thing about grace is that you can give away what you haven't gotten."* Some of the biblical examples that Trent and Smalley discuss include, for example, when Isaac blessed his son Jacob. They unpack important elements in administering the blessing to a loved one. These five elements include: 1) meaningful touch, 2) a spoken message, 3) attaching "high" value to the one being blessed, 4) picturing a special future for the one being blessed, and 5) an active commitment to fulfill the blessing (Trent & Smalley, 1982).

The Blessing seems to represent some of the characteristics of a secure autonomous attachment bond. The "picturing a special future for the one being blessed" component of the blessing that involves using a metaphor to picture a special future seems reminiscent of this concept (in Counted, 2016 research) of having participants use a metaphor to describe their experience of God. For example, one of my favorite metaphors that describes the personal nature of my experience of God and how I seek proximity to God is a Scripture that comes from Psalm 139:17. My favorite paraphrase of this Scripture comes from "Father's Love Letter" version which says, "*His thoughts towards you are countless as the sand on the seashore.*" Each time I have the blessing of going to the beach, I take a moment to grasp a handful of sand and let it run through my fingers. As I listen to the soothing sound of the ocean waves crashing against the shore, I am aware of the vastness of the ocean and of God, our Father, and I remind myself as the sand slips through my fingers, and as I gaze at the seashore filled with countless grains of sand . . . I remind myself that, "His thoughts towards me are countless." A tremendous feeling of peace and love wash over me as I contemplate the number of grains of sand on the seashore and how God's thoughts towards me are countless just as are those grains of sand that are flowing through my fingers. This experiences involves both God concept and God image. It involves concept in that I am cognitively aware of what God's Word says, and also God image, because the powerful context and experimental nature of feeling the sand, hearing the soothing sound of the waves, and seeing the vastness of the blue ocean help me to feel aware of his vastness and the lavishness of his love for me. Thus, there is both a cognitive and affective experience. This is the image that most often comes to mind and the setting in which I imagine myself when seeking proximity and closeness to God. Seeking proximity to God and engaging in mindfulness may involve being aware of his presence continually and meditating on it throughout the day.

Counted (2016), in his qualitative research, shared examples of how participants described their relationship with God to indicate proximity seeking by including some examples such as: "I think I've got a good relationship with God it is a personal relationship . . ." (Counted, 2016, p. 324). He shares that examples such as this illustrate that people use "symbolic language to describe their relationship with God" (Counted, 2016, p. 324), which fulfills one of the requirements for a relationship to be considered an attachment relationship. In addition, Counted found that proximity seeking and closeness to God looked different for different people. Some participants noted an enhanced sense of closeness to God when out in nature (Counted, 2016).

When people have a history of insecure relationships with attachment figures, research shows this often manifests in their relationship with God. These individuals had a connection with God and sought closeness to Him and was revealed by their words such as "close," "secure," and "trusting" (Counted, 2016, p. 325).

One saddening finding of the research Counted conducted was the idea that when individuals with an insecure attachment style discussed their relationship with God, they revealed they felt connected to God, but when the nature of their bond was examined, attachment conflicts were revealed and came out in "emotionally laden decibels" (Counted, 2016, p. 325). Counted's research took a closer look at these findings. One dynamic they uncovered was the theme, "connected but worried about abusing love by putting God aside," (Counted, 2016, p. 325). This theme was illustrated in the narrative of a participant who they call Andy. Andy identified himself as a Pentecostal who highly valued his relationship with God and said it was of utmost importance to him. However, Andy also confessed, "I would worry in my relationship with God . . . especially when I sin . . ." Researchers found that this reveals the implication that God may not be happy with him. The researcher shared, "Hence negative relationship experience with God are sustained here because of the moral demands of a stern, patriarchal God, whose actions are regarded in terms of purification, edification, and retribution" (Counted, 2016, p. 326).

Another participant had a connection to God, but also worried that she disappointed God. Another theme the research revealed is, "connected but no personal relationship with God" (Counted, 2016, p. 327). She revealed she is worried that she was trying to impress people and putting them before God.

"Connected but not strong enough" was a third theme revealed in the interviews. This was manifested by a participant's named Charlie's and her fear that she may go back to the world and talked about an attack which exhibits what Counted refers to as religious language as a response to God-attachment anxiety.

The emergence of the response to separation and loss was also discussed. Participants who went through a separation during early childhood looked to their relationship with God to compensate.

Much of the research on attachment to God has been conducted on adult samples; however, some has been conducted on child samples. In a study conducted on 7–12-year-olds in Finland, Taminen (1994) reported secure children felt closer to God during times of distress (such as emergencies and loneliness). Cassiba, Granqvist, and Costantini (2011) conducted a study on 71 maternal-child dyads and they found that children of securely attached mothers ranked God as closer during attachment activating situations. This was tested by hearing scenarios about a fictional child. Some scenarios were neutral and some scenarios were attachment activating. During attachment activating/stressful situations, the secure participants (mean age 7.5) ranked God closer to the fictional character than the children with an insecure status. The most interesting finding, and perhaps important for religious mothers, was that according to the research findings (Cassiba, Granqvist, and Costantini, 2013), children's ranking of God's closeness to them revealed that the sense of closeness to God was independent of parental religiosity. They found that rather children's attachment classification was linked to their mother's attachment security. In other words, a child's sense of God's closeness was associated with his or her mother's sensitivity and availability and independent of her religiosity.

GOD AS SECURE BASE

"No concept within the attachment framework is more central to Developmental psychiatry than that of the secure base."

— (Bowlby, 1988, p. 163-164)

© Kim Howell/Shutterstock.com

Now that we have discussed some of the research on God attachment, the process of seeking proximity to God, and finding comfort in him as a safe haven, let's now look at conceptualizing our relationship with God as our secure base.

The secure base and safe haven concept are interrelated and work in a reciprocal nature. A child needs the safe haven to come to during times of distress and a child also needs a secure base as a launching pad to explore from (Jones & Cassidy, 2014). Thus, reflecting back on the Scripture discussed in the safe haven section, recall that Dr. Jefferson reminded us Jesus called them to be with Him (safe haven) and then He sent them out (from that place of "being with" they went out into the world to share the gospel).

CONCLUDING THOUGHTS

And as He sends us, and as we go, we are the extension of His hands and arms. As we rest in knowing that He is our safe haven and secure base as clinicians, we can help our clients sift through their early attachment experiences, their God image, God concept, and capacity to relate to the Father Heart of God as our Divine Attachment Figure (please visit www.fathersloveletter. com for a powerful video illustrating the Father's heart, that safe haven to share with clients as appropriate, it is translated into over 100 languages).

CHAPTER 12 SUMMARY

In order to conceptualize God as an attachment figure in light of the definition of the term in the research literature, our relationship with him should be characterized by four requirements. These requirements include: 1) one must be able to seek proximity to God, 2) one must be able to conceptualize God as a safe haven, 3) One must be able to conceptualize God as secure base, and 4) He must be perceived as stronger and wiser (Cassidy, 2016). However, those that have experienced psychological insults and/or low/high grade trauma may need to do some work around cognitive experiences of God called God concepts and emotional experiences of God called God images before working on strengthening attachment to God. Moriarity's work on God Image is discussed. There are some other interesting findings in the research literature related to attachment to God. Some findings are discussed here such as the idea that strong maternal attachment sensitivity is associated with a child's perceived closeness to God, and this is independent of a mother's religiosity. The ideas of relating to God as a secure base, a safe haven, and seeking proximity to God are all discussed in detail along with Scriptures and examples. Dr. George Jefferson, Counselor Education and Supervision professor at Regent University's retirement email is shared to illustrate the reciprocal concept of the secure base and safe haven, and the parallel between Jesus calling his disciples to "be with" him before he sent them out was also discussed.

Recommended Readings

"Keep reading it is one of the most marvelous adventures that anyone can have."

— *Lloyd Alexander*

Each time I teach an intensive class where online students come in for a week-long intensive (this is where we are in the classroom from approximately 8am–5pm each day for a week and have pre-work to prepare for the class and post-work following the class), on the last day of class students ask me for a book list of texts I would recommend that may be consistent with a Christian worldview. Some have even given the particularly difficult challenge of selecting a top three! As one of my colleagues, Dr. George Jefferson used to say, "we cannot teach others anything, but rather lead them to the Lord and his Holy Spirit who is the giver of all truth." He liked to quote George MacDonald, who said, "No teacher should strive to make men think as he thinks, but to lead them to the living Truth, to the Master himself, of whom alone they can learn anything, who will make them in themselves know what is true by the very seeing of it."

So, with George MacDonald and George Jefferson words in mind, and as we close out the last chapter of this textbook, I always recommend seeking the Giver of all Truth. There are so many unknowns in life, and with what we do know, we need a degree of epistemic humility, ironically "knowing" that even our sense of knowing is not untouched by the fall, and so flawed.

Even so, the following texts and authors have contributed much to my conceptualization of attachment and have shared great content that I would recommend for anyone wanting to understand more on the topic.

1. ***Attachments* by Tim Clinton and Gary Sibcy**.

   I recommend starting with this book. It is written in a compelling way and is congruent with the research literature. Dr. Tim Clinton, the President of the American Association of Christian Counselors, approaches the topic from a Christian worldview and much experience in the field. Dr. Gary Sibcy, his co-author, is uniquely trained as an LPC and a clinical psychologist, offering the best of both worlds. He has also served as the director of Liberty University's doctoral program and brings much knowledge to the topic area. These authors address the topic of attachment in a compelling and engaging way that will keep you hanging onto the book.

2. **Articles by Kirkpatrick and Granqvist**.

   You will see these authors in the reference list of this book and cited all throughout the literature on God attachment. They have been key players in looking at spirituality in conjunction with attachment literature. I recommend perusing through their articles and reading their contributions.

3. **Mary Main and her colleagues C. George and N. Kaplan's work (assessment & manual available via training)**.

   They have developed a gold star attachment assessment known as the Adult Attachment Interview or AAI for short. There is a manual that corresponds with the training for the AAI that is an unpublished manuscript. One must pursue training to gain access to the text. The training is very rigorous and labor intensive, but the assessment and the text provide much insight into the measurement and evaluation of attachment, and I highly recommend it (for those interested and wanting to gain additional certifications and training).

   George, C., Kaplan, N., & Main, M. (1985). *The Adult Attachment Interview*. Unpublished manuscript, University of California at Berkeley.

4. Bob Marvin was a student of Mary Ainsworth. Mary Ainsworth was a student of John Bowlby, and John Bowlby is considered the Father of Attachment! Bob Marvin has developed a training and a powerful conceptual model of attachment called, "The Circle of Security" (Marvin, 2016, personal communication). He unpacks how the attachment system gets activated and the dynamics of seeking a secure base/safe haven, exploring, and recharging.

There are many more excellent sources on attachment and related topics, but the above listed sources are texts or authors that I have found especially helpful. Please see our reference list for more helpful sources.

May the Lord bless your continued studies on attachment, your counseling ministry, and your personal journey. The best is yet to be.

References

Amen, D. (2011). *The Amen Solution*. New York: Random House.

Bowlby, J. (1984). John Bowlby Attachment and Loss. Lifespan Learning Institute. Downloaded from: https://www.youtube.com/watch?v=VAAmSqv2GV8

Burns, D. (2008). *Feeling Good Together: The secret to making troubled relationships work*. New York: Random House.

Cassidy, J. (2016). The nature of the child's ties. In J. Cassidy & P. R. Shaver (Eds.), Handbook of attachment: Theory, research and clinical applications (pp. 3–20). New York: Guilford Press.

Cassidy, J. & Shaver, P. (2016). *Handbook of Attachment: Theory, Research, and Clinical Practice*. 3rd edition. New York, New York: The Guilford Press.

Cicchetti, D. and Barnett, D. (1991) Attachment Organization in Maltreated Preschoolers, *Development and Psychopathology* 3: 397–411.

Clinton, T. & Sibcy, G. (2009). *Attachments: Why you love, feel and act the way you do*. Thomas Nelson.

Counted, V. (2016). God as an Attachment Figure A case study of the God attachment language and God concepts of anxiously attached Christian youths in South Africa. p. 316–346. *Journal of Spirituality in Mental Health*. Volume 18, Issue 4.

Crowell, J. & Owens, G. (1998) *Manual for The Current Relationship Interview And Scoring System*. Version 4. Retrieved (September 9, 2017) from http://ww.psychology.sunysb.edu/attachment/ measures/content/cri_manual.pdf.

Feddern Donbaek, D., & Elklit, A. (2014). A validation of the Experiences in Close Relationships-Relationship Structures scale (ECR-RS) in adolescents. *Attachment & Human Development*, 16(1), 58–76. doi:10.1080/14616734.2013.850103

Feeney, J. A. (2016). Adult Romantic Attachment: Developments in the study of couple relationships. In Cassidy, J. & Shaver, P. *Handbook of Attachment: Theory, Research, and Clinical Applications.* New York: Guilford Press.

Foster, R. (2003). *Celebration of Discipline: The Path to Spiritual Growth.* New York: Harper Collins.

Garzon, F., & Ford, K. (2016). Adapting mindfulness for conservative Christians. *Journal of Psychology and Christianity, 35*(3), 263–268. Retrieved from http://ezproxy.liberty.edu/login?url=https://search-proquest-com.ezproxy.liberty.edu/docview/1869927867?accountid=12085

Goleman, D. (1995). *Emotional Intelligence.* New York: Bantam Books.

Gottman, J. (2001). *The Relationship Cure.* New York: Crown.

Gottman, J. & Clinton, T. (2013). *The Impact of Physiological Flooding.* Gottman Institute. https://www.youtube.com/watch?v=X2s0KvztrLo

Greely, A. & Hout, M. (2006). Happiness and Lifestyle among Conservative Christians. *The Truth about Conservative Christians*, 1, 150–161.

Harrichand, J., Knight, A.M., & Captari, D. (2017). The Role of EI in Preventing Counselor Burnout. Virginia Counselors Association Journal.

Haslam, S.A., Jetten, J., Postmes, T., & Haslam, C. (2009). Social identity, health and well-being: An emerging agenda for applied psychology. *Applied Psychology, 58*(1), 1–23.

Hawkins, R. Sibcy, G., Warren, S., & Knight, A. (In Press). *Empathic Counseling Skills.* Dubuque, IA: Kendall-Hunt Publishing Company.

Hummer, R. A., Rogers, R. G., Nam, C. B., & Ellison, C. G. (1999). Religious involvement and US adult mortality. *Demography*, 36(2), 273–285.

Ironson, G., Solomon, G. F., Balbin, E.G., O'Cleirigh, C., George, A., Kumar, M. (2002). The Ironson-Woods Spirituality/Religiousness Index is associated with long survival, health behaviors, less distress, low cortisol in people with HIV/AIDS. Annals of Behavioral Medicine, 24(1), 34–48.

Katie, B. (2002). *Loving What Is: Four questions that can change your life.* New York: Harmony Books.

Kavaler-Adler, S. (2014). *The Klein-Winnicott Dialectic: Transformative New Metapsychology and Interactive Clinical Theory.* Karnac Books.

Knight, A. M. (2009). *The Effective Practices in Counseling Skills Training and its Relationship with Emotional Intelligence.* Virginia Beach, VA: Proquest Digital Dissertations, Regent University.

Main & Goldwyn (1980).

Main, M., & Goldwyn, R. (in press). Predicting rejection of her infant from mother's representation of her own experiences: A preliminary report. *International Journal of Child Abuse and Neglect.*

Main, M., Hess, E. & Siegel, D. (2010). *Adult Attachment Interview with Mary Main. Lifespan Learning LA.* YouTube Video.

Main, M., Kaplan, N., & Cassidy, J. (1985). Security in Infancy, Childhood, and Adulthood: A Move to the Level of Representation. *Monographs of the Society for Research in Child Development*, 50(1/2), 66–104. doi:10.2307/3333827

Marvin, B. (2013). *Dr. Bob Marvin on Attachment and Developmental Pathway to Healing.* The Ainsworth Attachment Center and Circle of Security. YouTube.

Marvin, R. & Seagroves, W. (2017). *Attachment, Trauma, and the Circle of Security.* Continuing Education Presentation at Liberty University.

McCullough, J. P., Lord, B. D., Martin, A. M., Conley, K. A., Schramm, E., & Klein, D. N. (2011). The significant other history: An interpersonal-emotional history procedure used with the early-onset chronically depressed patient. *American Journal of Psychotherapy*, 65(3), 225–48. Retrieved from http://ezproxy.liberty.edu/login?url=https://search-proquest-com.ezproxy.liberty.edu/docview/903284191?accountid=12085

Merriam-Webster Dictionary. (1828). https://www.merriam-webster.com/dictionary/syncretism

Mishra, S. K, Togneri, E., Tripathi, B., Trikmahi, B. (2017). Spirituality and Religiosity and its Role in Health and Diseases. *Journal of Religion and Health.* Volume 56, issue 4, p. 1282–1301.

Neborsky, R. (2006). Brain, mind, and dyadic change processes. *Journal of Clinical Psychology*, 62(5), 523–538. doi:10.1002/jclp.20246

Pedersen, G., Eikenæs, I., Urnes, Ø., Skulberg, G. M., & Wilberg, T. (2015). Experiences in Close Relationships—Psychometric properties among patients with personality disorders. *Personality & Mental Health*, 9(3), 208–219. doi:10.1002/pmh.1298

Penberthy, J. K. (In Progress). *Persistent Depressive Disorders.* Germany: Hogrefe Publishing.

Petrides, K. V. and Furnham, A. (2006), The Role of Trait Emotional Intelligence in a Gender-Specific Model of Organizational Variables1. *Journal of Applied Social Psychology*, 36: 552–569. doi:10.1111/j.0021-9029.2006.00019.x

Petrides, K. V., Pita, R., & Kokkinaki, F. (2007). The location of trait emotional intelligence in personality factor space. *British Journal Of Psychology*, 98(2), 273–289. doi:10.1348/000712606X120618

Pichurin V.V. (2017). Coping Strategies and Psychological Readiness of Students for Professional work. *Pedagogìka, Psihologìâ ta Mediko-bìologìčnì Problemi Fìzičnogo Vihovannâ ì Sportu.*

Saarakallio, S. (2010). Music as Emotional Self-Regulation throughout Adulthood. *Psychology of Music*. 39 (3), 307–327.

Sibcy, G. A. & Knight, A. M. (2011). Emotional Intelligence, Attachment Theory, and Neuroscience: Implications for Counselors. AACC World Conference Presentation, Nashville, TN.

Sibcy, G. & Knight, A. (2017). Emotional Intelligence and the Attachment Behavioral System. In Summers, R. (Eds.). *Social Psychology: How Other People Influence Our Thoughts and Actions*. (59–86). Santa Barbara, CA: Greenwood.

Sibcy, G. A. & Knight, A. M. (2016). Chapter published in 2016 in R. Summers (Ed.), Advances in Experimental Social Psychology. Santa Barbara, CA ABC-CLIO publishers.

Sibcy, G. A. & Knight, A. M. (In Progress). CBASP treatment and AAI Classification: Single Case Design Research.

Siegel, D. (2009). *Dr. Dan Siegel—On Making Sense of Your Past*. Psych Alive. https://www.youtube.com/watch?v=w0sAROt7gSU

Spangler, G., & Grossmann, K. (1993). Biobehavioral Organization in Securely and Insecurely Attached Infants. *Child Development*, 64(5), 1439–1450. doi:10.2307/1131544

Steele, M. & Steele, H. (2016). Ten Clinical Uses of the Adult Attachment Interview. In Steele, M. & Steele, H. (Eds.). *Clinical Applications of the Adult Attachment Interview*. New York: The Guilford Press.

Thompson, C. (2010). *Anatomy of the Soul: Surprising Connections between Neuroscience and Spiritual Practices That Can Transform Your Life and Relationships*. Carol Stream, IL: Tyndale Momentum.

Wilmer, D. & Brady, P. (2002). *Rose is Rose*. Go Comics. Downloaded from: http://www.gocomics.com/roseisrose

Appendix

CODING RESOURCES

Dean Dozier (certified reliable coder)
Adult Attachment Interview Coder
Her website is: www.aaicoding.com
Her email is deandozier@gmail.com
She provides AAI coding services.

Resource website for Anita M. Knight (certified reliable coder) & Gary Sibcy

You can also visit www.anitaknight.com for more resources on attachment, EI and AAI coding.

CPSIA information can be obtained
at www.ICGtesting.com
Printed in the USA
LVOW06s1215201017
552972LV00001B/1/P

9 781524 949587